THE HOUR OF DEGENERATION

"When I Was Daily with You in the Temple,
Ye Stretched Forth No Hands Against Me:
But This Is Your Hour, and the Power of
Darkness." (Luke 22:53; KJV)

Twyman Preston Joyner D.D.

WESTBOW°
PRESS
A DIVISION OF THOMAS NELSON
& ZONDERVAN

WestBow Press books may be ordered through
booksellers or by contacting:

WestBow Press
A Division of Thomas Nelson & Zondervan
1663 Liberty Drive
Bloomington, IN 47403
www.westbowpress.com
1 (866) 928-1240

ISBN: 978-1-4908-4308-7 (sc)

Library of Congress Control Number: 2014911976

Printed in the United States of America.

WestBow Press rev. date: 7/9/2014

Contents

In Dedication

I dedicate this book to my spiritual mother in the Lord; Evangelist Bertha E. Jones (1906-2000); she taught me wisdom, love and compassion. Thank you Lord Jesus for bringing her into my life—she definitely made a difference in me. I miss her ever so much.

A Concise Acknowledgement

To my Theological Bible Group in Oklahoma City, OK

Thank you for all your prayers, encouragement and support

Much love and great wisdom to you all

A Special Word of Gratitude

I would like to thank my dear sister, Dr. Shirley A. (Joyner) Wilson-Beckwith and her husband Jamez Beckwith for their love and ministry to the Joyner family throughout the years. Your service, dedication and loyalty are greatly appreciated. We will never forget what you have done for us as a family. Jamez you have taught me how to show respect and romantic love to my good wife Wanda, because of the love and honor you have shown towards my sister. Shirley your guidance through the years has aided me well and I am so blessed to have such a smart and loving sister as yourself. We Joyner's are truly a blessed people and we owe the Lord Jesus all of the glory, honor, praise and a life of dedication devoted only to Him.

Preface

I thank God for the abilities He has given me to see and observe the times in which we live. This book is written just for that purpose. Paul said in Ephesians 5:16, "Redeem [save] or make-up for lost time as well as making good use of your time and opportunities given, since the times in which we live are so immoral, wicked and debauched" (paraphrased by T.P. Joyner). If he said this in his times, then our modern times must be nearing the pinnacle of evil and immorality. From the time of Adam and Eve to the time of Noah (*Noe*), sin went from its infant state to maturity and God destroyed all living (accept the fishes and sea animals), but preserved Noah, his family and some of the domestic and wild life animals and insects present in the Ark (Gen. 6-8).

Jesus reveals to us in Luke 17: 22-30 that before His return the world's sinful state would be synonymous with the days of Noah and Lot [who dwelled in Sodom (Gen. 19: 1-30)], thus the people would be going about their business as usual (cf. Matthew 24:34-44). However, [sin's] deteriorating effect on this world will someday close-out and Christ will return "with power and great glory" [Matt. 24:30], putting an end to this world's system that is under

Satan's authority (Eph. 2: 1-3). It is my intentions to get the reader to see that the times in which we live are serious and critical. These are dangerous times and we must be alert—watching and praying (Mark 13: 33ff). We must become the true people of God [the household of faith—that is in Christ Jesus] and not just following after every wind and doctrine taught by false prophets and false teachers. It is my prayer that this book enlightens and gives the reader more knowledge about the "perilous times" in which we live. This is a degenerating hour and the so-called Christians must wake-up to the fact that if we don't change our ways and turn away from the evils of this world, many will be lost due to our indiscretions or lack of godly wisdom. Always remember ignorance is not bliss, and what you don't know can hurt you, however, this one saying is precisely the truth—and that is, "the fear of the Lord is the beginning of wisdom" (Psa. 111: 10; Prov. 1: 7; 9:10).

Moses Wrote These Words In Genesis 6:11-12:

"The earth was depraved *and* putrid in God's sight, and the land was filled with violence (desecration, infringement, outrage, assault, and lust for power). And God looked upon the world and saw how degenerate, debased, *and* vicious it was, for all humanity had corrupted their way upon the earth *and* lost their true direction" (Amp).

Chapter One

Degeneration And
The
Apostasy

In this chapter we will be defining and analyzing the word *degeneration*—researching its etymology or word origin and other salient points about degeneration in this modern era, as well as the present apostasy of Christianity [which is progressively increasing] and its word meaning. The word degeneration derived from the root word degenerate, which literally means to be inferior to one's ancestry or to not meet the quality or standard of one's origin. From the late 1500's Latin *degenerationem and degeneratus, we get the phase de genere*, from *de* + *genus* (gen. *generis*) "birth, descent" (http://www.etymonline.com/index.php?term=degenerate).

Degeneration connotes "deterioration" which means to become rotten and to decay or to diminish in quality and grow worse in character, and values. A degenerate is one that is a corrupt, perverted, immoral, deviant reprobate. Therefore, in our society today the degenerates have become the leaders of this modern world. That which was considered evil and wrong and antagonistic against God is now pure, good and up-right in the sight of human beings.

However, those who seek moral righteousness and acquiesces with godliness are considered as religious bigots, who are judgmental of those who have different views then they do, in which they are very intolerant of others beliefs and perspectives. The Bible speaks clear to us that in the last days the good will be hated and that which is corrupt will be acceptable. Paul cites this in II Timothy 3: 1-5:

> *"In the last days (the closing of time as we know it), there will be a time within that period that is designated for a time of terror—dangers, great distress that is unbearable with great turmoil. People's selfishness will be out of control [thinking only of themselves or 'what's in it for them']. Money, greed and wealth will be their main focus and first priority.*
>
> *Therefore, they will be egotistical narcissistic braggers who are hated for their arrogance. They will be rude, obnoxious and offensive, not obeying their parents, unappreciative and unthankful, denying God's righteousness and holy living defiantly; preferring to live sacrilegiously. These cold-blooded merciless people are not willing to*

engage into an armistice, but will increase their ruthless attacks against godliness and true holiness.

Thus they will not hesitate to make false malicious statements to damage the reputation of others, [making trouble with their lies and deceit]. Due to their antagonisms, they will be hot-headed and mean-spirited, lacking in scruples and principles—their behavior will be out of control and intensely violent. Therefore, they will strongly dislike good and those who practice righteous living, as well as double-crossing those who are loyal to them with their conceited reckless injudicious life style.

Hence, these reprobates will be superfluously voluptuous in their sexual delights which are worthless enjoyments compared to loving their Maker [which is God Almighty]. I greatly warn you without hesitation, to stay away from such people and have nothing to do with them. Even if they do appear to act religious and pious they are deniers of its power to totally transform lives, and that power is pleasing in the sight of God" (paraphrased by T.P. Joyner to make salient points about our subject).

It seems or it appears that as the years go by that the degenerates are growing at a rapid pace, and the ways of righteousness are being suppressed. People are losing their moral values, and the standards of truth and holiness are being condemned or censored and put down by the standards of humanism. As secular humanism grows godliness is seen as useless and futile. While some declare that the Bible is outdated and that some scriptures were embellished later—causing biblical error. This is causing people to give-up on God's Word, by which the animal instinct of the human nature is now taking center stage and a Holy Spirit lead life is now becoming a thing of the past in today's contemporary society. The Amplified Bible explicitly reveals the humanistic ways and its secularism (which only concern is the energy of the flesh). Paul admonishes the assembly at Colossae fervently:

> *"So kill (deaden, deprive of power) the evil desire lurking in your members [those animal impulses and all that is earthly in you that is employed in sin]: sexual vice, impurity, sensual appetites, unholy desires, and all greed and covetousness, for that is idolatry (the deifying of self and other created things instead of God)"* [Colossians 3: 5; Amp (we will explore more into secular humanism in chapter two of this book)].

One thing is very true in this modern age in which we live, and that is, that the degenerates are growing even more and more defiant against God's righteousness [with an *in* your face type of attitude]. People are battling within themselves whether to do that which is scrupulous verses that which is an abomination or detestable in God's sight. In most cases society pressures people to do what is antagonistic and hostile to God's standards (His values and principles). People in the *so-called* church are beginning to acquiesce and accept immorality within Christian groups.

Why do I say *"so-called church?"* I say this because Christian morality is weakening and their love for God's word is dissipating. Christians are into horoscopes, dabbling in witchcraft, participating in false prophesies (see chapter four on Prophet-lying), same sex relationships, drug abuse, alcoholism, lying, stealing and the list goes on. Through these examples, we see that degeneration equates apostasy in this modern Christian era [Christians are not advocating what Jesus and the apostles taught—they are doing their own thing—sort of speak]. What happened to true holiness, righteousness and faith towards God? It is now becoming a thing of the past.

Apostasy—

In this hour of degeneration we see a decline in church ethics and morals. The contemporary Church ethics compared to the ethics of the saints of God (*ekklesia*) of antiquity. For example, many in the so-called Pentecostal/Charismatic/Word of Faith movements preach and teach against what they call a religious spirit, how they are staying with what the apostles teach. Yet they are still way out of line and off base with what the apostles taught. The apostles did not teach tithing, robbing the people of their finances for material gain and profit, nor did they teach prosperity through seed faith giving—that is giving to a person's so-called ministry and God will prosper you financially (for more information on financial Christianity refer to my book "His Mighty Word of Power" which addresses this subject in chapters eleven and thirteen).

The apostle Paul admonished Timotheus in I Timothy 6: 3-11 to stay away from those who would bring shame on the Gospel with unwholesome teaching:

> *"Therefore, If anyone teach anything, other than the Gospel of Christ [the doctrine that is in harmony with devoting one's life to God, which emphasizes clean-living], that person should be considered arrogant and self-conceited in their ignorance or lacking of knowledge of God's word. This person takes pleasure in gloomy depressing arguments, clashing over controversies and fighting over words, which produce contentions and discord; being envious of others, with cruelty and causing divisions—using foul language and disparaging people, as well as being dishonorably suspicious of others and having long drawn out power struggles with exhausting dialogues that are irksome.*
>
> *Having continuous hostilities among the people who are tainted and devoid of truth [God's truth], who envisions righteous living as a way to obtain money [a source of revenue—as a business for profit and financial gain]. Please, extract yourself from*

this behavior [have nothing to do with this]. Even though they are making a lot of money, we should be devoutly contented in our faith [which gives great satisfaction], which is far more rewarding in its abundance and benefits.

Therefore, we did not bring anything into this natural world and it's certain that we will not be able to take anything with us when we die [or pass from this natural life]. Now, if we have the necessities of life [which is food and clothing], let us be happy with contentment and gratitude to God. However, those people who hunger after riches [who crave after money and wealth], tumble and are lured into traps of folly and ungodly desires leading to their demise, thrusting them to their doom, to die in misery.

Now, loving money is the very base and cause of all that is evil, which opposes God. It is because of this love for money that some of you have apostatized from faith in Christ to the love for material gain; your mental emotional behavior has become very intense, seriously inflicting yourselves. Lastly, I admonish you O people of God to go after righteous living and avoid this ungodliness, fearing the Lord with a Christlike life, steadfast in the faith, walking in God's loving kindness and tender heartfelt mercies daily" (paraphrased by T.P. Joyner to make salient points about our subject).

Wow! Paul makes an explicit relevant statement for our present times when he stated this in verse 10:

> *"Now, loving money is the very base and cause of all that is evil, which opposes God. It is because of this love for money that some of you have apostatized from faith in Christ to the love for material gain; your mental emotional behavior has become very intense, seriously inflicting yourselves."*

This modern age of preachers and church laity [so-called] are so caught-up in trying to become rich and some are getting rich, and then apostasy sets in, and they wander "from the faith" with their consciences (scruples or ethical principles) and mental behavior turns seriously for the worse, unable to discern the truth from a lie (I Timothy 4: 1-2; see the next segment on *Doctrines of Devils —Demons are Teachers*). Even though they are still active in Christian church ministries and leadership, their Christian ethics have weakened and their morals have dwindled because of their love for money and materialism.

Doctrines of Devils—Demons are Teachers

Paul admonished Timothy [*and I paraphrase*] that "The Holy Spirit speaks very clear (unequivocally) and specifically, proclaiming that at the conclusion of time as we know it (the final days or the end of time), There will be a falling away (apostasy) from faith in Jesus and the teachings of God's

Word, due to demonical teaching (or a demonic dogma), that has deluded (hoodwinked, tricked, deceived) people into pretenders of the faith. Whose consciences (ethics or the sense of what is right and wrong) are branded with lies and deceit (Tim. 4:1-2)."

This is so relevant today and prevalent; people accepting paganism and heathenism in their so-called churches. There is no more standing-up for righteousness and true holiness; the so-called Christians are saying that "everything is okay, we can't judge anyone; we must love everybody—this is God's place not ours." This is just a cop-out, or failing to take on the responsibilities that God has given to His elect. The so-called churches are allowing homosexuality and same-sex marriage (there are even homosexual churches), adultery, fornication, drug addiction, alcoholism, gambling (playing the lottery and patronizing casinos), and philosophies of humans in place of theology proper, prophet-lying and false prophets.

People are afraid to confront preachers who deliberately lie to them to get their money. The gospel that is being preached is not the good news that Jesus revealed to us (*because many are teaching a demonical dogma*). God has *entrusted* us (the believers) with gifts and talents to bring correction to errors, by which will unite earth-born humanity to *pursue* or engage in habitual fellowship with God Almighty, thus being proficient and dexterous in "every good work" (2 Tim. 3: 16-17). We are the Body of Christ and Christ is the Word of God (*Logos*). If this be the case then we are to proclaim His Words to this wicked generation without compromise. Many of us know absolutely nothing about the patristic writings of the Early Christian Fathers after the Apostles. It is evident, because if one would read these writings, one would never ever call themselves apostles, because the Early Christian Fathers taught that the apostleship had ended and that they were *not* apostles—they had great respect for the apostles who ordained them as bishops and overseers.

The False Teaching Which Refers To the End-time Great Revival

Many believe that there will be a *great revival* before the Second Advent of Jesus Christ (the Parousia). I beg to differ—I even I myself use to proclaim the same exact thing. But this is not in line with scripture nor is it the truth. It is just human desire for God to manifest His presence supernaturally to this wicked contemporary age. Down through the ages of time God has sent revival after revival and reawakening after reawakening, and has manifested His presence time and time again to the *so-called church*, and humanity has still found a way to foul things up and causes the word of God to be of none effect as the end of time approaches.

Once again let us revisit 1 Timothy 4:1-2 from the Message Bible (MSG) this time, to hear what the apostle Paul (who was the most active of the apostles on this subject) had to say about the *apostasy* of the latter days.

"The Spirit makes it clear that as time goes on, some are going to give up on the faith and chase after demonic illusions put forth by professional liars. These liars have lied so well and for so long that they've lost their capacity for truth"

Then Paul goes on to say this to the assembly at Thessalonica:

*"But relative to the coming of our Lord Jesus Christ (the Messiah) and our gathering together to [meet] Him, we beg you, brethren, Not to allow your minds to be quickly unsettled or disturbed or kept excited or alarmed, whether it be by some [pretended] revelation of [the] Spirit or by word or by letter [alleged to be] from us, to the effect that the day of the Lord has [already] arrived and is here. **Let no one deceive or beguile you in any way, for that day will not come except the apostasy comes first [unless the predicted great falling away of those who have professed to be Christians has come]**, and the man of lawlessness (sin) is revealed, who is the son of doom (of perdition), Who opposes and exalts himself so proudly and insolently against and over all that is called God or that is worshiped, [even to his actually] taking his seat in the temple of God, proclaiming that he himself is God"* (II Thessalonians 2:1-4; Amp; **bold emphasis added**).

The *apostasia* (in the Greek) connotes; to forsake or defection (to reject the ways of God and abandon one's allegiance to Christ and His teachings). There are some who will withdraw from the faith and some have and are doing so at this very moment, even though they are still calling themselves Christians. The closet and openly [so-called "gay"] homosexuals (sodomites and lesbians) are now taking center stage in the *so-called* church. Many church organizations are allowing these reprobates to be leaders in their congregations (see Romans 1: 25ff). Some of the so-called bishops and pastors make jokes and say that "the gays have always been part of the church and this is nothing new (they are our music ministers). We must accept and embrace them in our churches as well."

This is deceptions and trickery that only Satan can muster—for it is he who has called up this wickedness. How can that which is antagonistic against God bless His people? Can darkness overpower light? Has good become evil and evil become righteousness and purity? The modern day so-called *church* cannot discern good from evil. This is a sad hour in which we live, because the earth [and the so-called church] is receiving Satan's beguiles instead of Jesus' and the apostles' instructions. They will not give an ear to sound doctrine or receive the clear messages of admonitions written to the *assemblies* from God's inspired word. Paul gives an unequivocal caveat in 2 Timothy 4: 1-5:

> *"I charge [you] in the presence of God and of Christ Jesus, Who is to judge the living and the*

dead, and by (in the light of) His coming and His kingdom: Herald and preach the Word! Keep your sense of urgency [stand by, be at hand and ready], whether the opportunity seems to be favorable or unfavorable. [Whether it is convenient or inconvenient, whether it is welcome or unwelcome, you as preachers of the Word are to show people in what way their lives are wrong.] And convince them, rebuking and correcting, warning and urging and encouraging them, being unflagging and inexhaustible in patience and teaching. For the time is coming when [people] will not tolerate (endure) sound and wholesome instruction, but, having ears itching [for something pleasing and gratifying], they will gather to themselves one teacher after another to a considerable number, chosen to satisfy their own liking and to foster the errors they hold; and will turn aside from hearing the truth and wander off into myths and man-made fictions. As for you, be calm and cool and steady, accept and suffer unflinchingly every hardship, do the work of an evangelist, fully perform all the duties of your ministry" (Amp).

It is amazing to me how much truth these scriptures divulge. It is also amazing to me that people can carry a Bible and read it and still not comprehend or get a handle on what is written in God's word. I believe that the manmade fictions have replaced the truths of the *Holy Writ*. However, when the truth is presented, the people in the so-called churches are offended and they cling to their sanctimonious traditions of manmade fictions and clichés instead of that which will give them life or set them free [which is the pure unadulterated (naked), inerrant and infallible Word of God].

Apostasy and the Early Christian Fathers (the Apostles)

This seed of apostasy began in first century Christianity due to the Gnostic heresies. However, for the first 200 years of Christian history the apostles and early Christian fathers were adamant when it came to schisms (party spirit) and dissentions within the assemblies (Galatians 5: 20). They preached unity in the faith and love (Eph. 4:13; 1John 4: 7ff; c.f. John 3:16-17). Jesus prayed these words to the Father concerning His apostles and the future disciples that would be birthed through them in John 17:

> *"Holy Father, keep in Your Name [in the knowledge of Yourself] those whom You have given Me, that they may be one as We [are one]"* (John 17:11; Amp).

Then He goes on to say this in verses 21-23:

> *"That they all may be one, [just] as You, Father, are in Me and I in You, that they also may be one in Us, so that the world may believe and be convinced that*

You have sent Me. I have given to them the glory and honor which You have given Me, that they may be one [even] as We are one: I in them and You in Me, in order that they may become one and perfectly united, that the world may know and [definitely] recognize that You sent Me and that You have loved them [even] as You have loved Me" (Amp).

The Views on Apostasy from Other Apostles besides Paul

Now, we have heard some of Paul's views on apostasy as well as Jesus' emphasis on unity. However, what do the other apostles in first century Christianity have to say about this most critical subject of, "dividing from the faith"?

Saint John's Warning against Docetism (A.D. 97)

The apostle John admonishing the saints with Cyria (the elect lady) to guard against Gnostics Docetism, the doctrine which advocated that Jesus did not come in the flesh [He was just a celestial illusion] (see 2 John1: 7).We know that this teaching is incorrect because after Jesus' resurrection He showed Himself to over five hundred people at one time (1 Cor. 15:3-8). He also appeared to Mary Magdalene (Mark 16: 9-11), Peter and James (the Lord's brother) individually as well as walked and ate with the two disciples whom He traveled with on the road to the village called Emmaus (Luke 24:13-35).

Later, He appeared to the ten [Thomas was not present] and then to the eleven apostles and John was an eye witness of both instances or accounts. Therefore, Luke 24: 36-43; c.f. John 20:24-29 reveals that Jesus appeared as terrestrial not in celestial form to His disciples. Theses scriptures acquiesce with John's statement, that the Lord did have a material body. Finally, let us not forget the mother of Jesus, Mary [who gave birth to Him] and all His immediate family and friends who shared His life from childhood to adulthood in Nazareth, as well as the Pharisees and Sadducees who opposed Him. There is no way that Jesus did not have a human body—Docetism is a ludicrous and preposterous doctrine.

John's Warnings against Apostasy

> *"Look to yourselves (take care) that you may not lose (throw away or destroy) all that we and you have labored for, but that you may [persevere until you] win and receive back a perfect reward [in full]. Anyone who runs on ahead [of God] and does not abide in the doctrine of Christ [who is not content with what He taught] does not have God; but he who continues to live in the doctrine (teaching) of Christ [does have God], he has both the Father and the Son" (2John 1:8-9; Amp).*

In the book of Revelation *[written A.D. 95]* Jesus discloses to John His concerns and admonitions toward the *seven assemblies.* It is amazing to me how that we are so easily to be deceived and forget the Lord's instructions and our devotion towards Him (c.f. Genesis 3).

To Ephesus:

"But I have this [one charge to make] against you: that you have left (abandoned) the love that you had at first [you have deserted Me, your first love]. Remember then from what heights you have fallen. Repent (change the inner man to meet God's will) and do the works you did previously [when first you knew the Lord], or else I will visit you and remove your lampstand from its place, unless you change your mind and repent" (Rev. 2:4-5; Amp).

To Smyrna:

"Be loyally faithful unto death [even if you must die for it], and I will give you the crown of life. He who is able to hear, let him listen to and heed what the Spirit says to the assemblies (churches). He who overcomes (is victorious) shall in no way be injured by the second death" (Rev. 2: 10b-11; Amp).

To Pergamum:

"Nevertheless, I have a few things against you: you have some people there who are clinging to the teaching of Balaam, who taught Balak to set a trap and a stumbling block before the sons of Israel, [to entice them] to eat food that had been sacrificed to

idols and to practice lewdness [giving themselves up to sexual vice] You also have some who in a similar way are clinging to the teaching of the Nicolaitans [those corrupters of the people] which thing I hate. Repent [then]! Or else I will come to you quickly and fight against them with the sword of My mouth" (Rev. 2: 14-16; Amp).

To Thyatira:

"But I have this against you: that you tolerate the woman Jezebel, who calls herself a prophetess [claiming to be inspired], and who is teaching and leading astray my servants and beguiling them into practicing sexual vice and eating food sacrificed to idols. But to the rest of you in Thyatira, who do not hold this teaching, who have not explored and known the depths of Satan, as they say—I tell you that I do not lay upon you any other [fresh] burden: Only hold fast to what you have until I come" (Rev. 2:20, 24, 25; Amp).

To Sardis:

"Rouse yourselves and keep awake, and strengthen and invigorate what remains and is on the point of dying; for I have not found a thing that you have done [any work of yours] meeting the requirements of My God or perfect in His sight. So call to mind the lessons you received and heard; continually lay them to heart and obey them, and repent. In case you will not rouse yourselves and keep awake and watch, I will come upon you like a thief, and you will not know or suspect at what hour

I will come. Yet you still have a few [persons'] names in Sardis who have not soiled their clothes, and they shall walk with Me in white, because they are worthy and deserving" (Rev. 3:2-4; Amp).

To Philadelphia:

"I am coming quickly; hold fast what you have, so that no one may rob you and deprive you of your crown" (Rev. 3:11; Amp).

To Laodicea:

"For you say, I am rich; I have prospered and grown wealthy, and I am in need of nothing; and you do not realize and understand that you are wretched, pitiable, poor, blind, and naked. Therefore I counsel you to purchase from Me gold refined and tested by fire, that you may be [truly] wealthy, and white clothes to clothe you and to keep the shame of your nudity from being seen, and salve to put on your eyes, that you may see. Those whom I [dearly and tenderly] love, I tell their faults and convict and convince and reprove and chasten [I discipline and instruct them]. So be enthusiastic and in earnest and burning with zeal and repent [changing your mind and attitude]" (Rev. 3:17-19; Amp).

If you notice out of the seven assemblies (*ekklesia*), Smyrna and Philadelphia were the only assemblies that did not have to repent for sin, only Smyrna was warned that persecution was coming [which was orchestrated by Satan]

(Rev. 2:10). However, the Lord still admonished them to be devotedly or dutifully faithful even until death [do not fall away or apostatize from the truth]. It appears that Jesus was and is very concerned about apostasy when it comes to His people. He reveals this concern to John very early in this revelation, signifying the urgency of the matter, because Christ knows the hearts [or the essence] of humankind (John 2:24-25).

St. Peter's Views on the Apostasy (A.D. 67)

Before Peter's death He was very adamant about the saints maintaining a habitual fellowship of true holiness and walking in right-standing with God. However, they should not entertain people (i.e. false prophets) of ungodliness and part take in their follies. The Christians should not again enmesh themselves in the "yokes of bondage" (Galatians 5:1), but maintain their steadfast walk *(biosis)* with Christ. These unrighteous carousers are only interested in the energy of the flesh and if the saints have company with them, they must beware, lest they may become entangle or caught in a snare, because of their ungodly enticements. In 2 Peter chapter two, we see some of the best admonitions and practical teachings to guard against apostasy:

> *"For if, after they have escaped the pollutions of the world through [the full, personal] knowledge of our Lord and Savior Jesus Christ, they again become entangled in them and are overcome, their*

last condition is worse [for them] than the first. For never to have obtained a [full, personal] knowledge of the way of righteousness would have been better for them than, having obtained [such knowledge], to turn back from the holy commandment which was [verbally] delivered to them. There has befallen them the thing spoken of in the true proverb, The dog turns back to his own vomit, and, The sow is washed only to wallow again in the mire" (2 Peter 2:20-22; Amp; cf. Proverbs 26:11).

In chapter three he makes this statement:

"Let me warn you therefore, beloved, that knowing these things beforehand, you should be on your guard, lest you be carried away by the error of lawless and wicked [persons and] fall from your own [present] firm condition [your own steadfastness of mind]. But grow in grace (undeserved favor, spiritual strength) and recognition and knowledge and understanding of our Lord and Savior Jesus Christ (the Messiah). To Him [be] glory (honor, majesty, and splendor) both now and to the day of eternity. Amen (so be it)" (2 Peter 3: 17-18; Amp)!

Jude's Views on the Apostasy (A.D. 75)

"Guard and keep yourselves in the love of God; expect and patiently wait for the mercy of our Lord

> *Jesus Christ (the Messiah)—[which will bring you]*
> *unto life eternal"* (Jude 1:20; Amp).

He goes on to say this in verse twenty-four:

> *"Now to Him Who is able to keep you without*
> *stumbling or slipping or falling, and to present [you]*
> *unblemished (blameless and faultless) before the*
> *presence of His glory in triumphant joy and exultation*
> *[with unspeakable, ecstatic delight]"* (Amp).

Jude concise letter was to admonish the saints with an apologetic plea "to contend or dispute for the faith" and to keep themselves in God's love—guarding against false teachings, as well as patiently awaiting the Parousia (the Second Coming of Christ) unto everlasting life—therefore, protecting themselves from apostasy and its enticements.

Second Century Christian Fathers on Apostasy (The Bishops)

As Christianity began to spread around the world in places like Germany, Libya, Egypt, Iberian Peninsula and the land of the Celts, the second Century Christian Fathers such as Ignatius, Polycarp, Justin Martyr, Irenaeus, Tertullian and other Ante-Nicene Fathers did all that they could to preserve the teachings of Jesus and the apostles. Irenaeus had this to say about universal (*katholikos*) Christian unity in his time:

"Having received this preaching and this faith, as I have said, the Church, although scattered in the whole world, carefully preserves it, as if living in one house. She believes these things [everywhere] alike, as if she had but one heart and one soul, and preaches them harmoniously, teaches them, and hands them down, as if she had but one mouth. For the languages of the world are different, but the meaning of the [Christian] tradition is one and the same." [http://www.ccel.org/ccel/richardson/fathers.xi.i.iii.html; *Early Church Fathers*; 360 Faith of the Church; 2nd paragraph]

Ignatius (Theophorus), Bishop of Antioch (birth [n.d.]; death c. 110)

There are some who believe that Ignatius was the child in Matthew 18:4-5 in which Jesus was alluding to. If this is the case, then, that means that he touched Jesus and affected Christian leadership of the second century and beyond. Before his execution in Rome, Bishop Ignatius made this statement to the assembly at Philadelphia:

"Keep your flesh as the temple of God, love unity, flee from divisions, be imitators of Jesus Christ, as was he also of his Father." [http://www.cumorah.com/index.php?target=outreach_articles&story_id=10; Loss of Apostolic Leadership and Revelation; 2nd paragraph]

Because of the loss of apostolic leadership at the close of the first century, Ignatius life was now coming to a close due to his imminent execution. He thought that in order to avoid the present "heretic poison," the people must stay in unity with their *Bishop, Elders and Deacons* to avoid apostasy. Therefore, Ignatius was the first to change the order of leadership in which the apostles had established [viz.; Apostles, Bishops (Elders or *presbyteros*), and Deacons] because of the cessation of the apostleship.

Polycarp the Bishop of Smyrna (c. 69-155)

Polycarp [who was martyred at age 86] was a devout student of the Apostle John, and with great passion and intensity he would warn the assemblies against heresies and apostasy—not only in Smyrna, but also in his famous letter of admonition to the Philippians, he made this statement:

> *"Wherefore gird up your loins and serve God in fear and truth, forsaking the vain and empty talking and the error of the many, for that ye have believed on Him that raised our Lord Jesus Christ from the dead and gave unto him glory and a throne on His right hand; unto whom all things were made subject that are in heaven and that are on the earth; to whom every creature that hath breath doeth service; who cometh as judge of quick and dead; whose blood God will require of them that*

are disobedient unto Him." [Polycarp 2:1; *JBL* translation; http://www.earlychristianwritings. com/text/ oshuap-lightfoot.html]

Irenaeus the Bishop of Lyons (ca. 125-202)

Irenaeus had this to say about heretics that were causing apostasy in his day:

"1. Certain men, rejecting the truth, are introducing among us false stories and vain genealogies, which serve rather to controversies, as the apostle said, than to God's work of building up in the faith. By their craftily constructed rhetoric they lead astray the minds of the inexperienced, and take them captive, corrupting the oracles of the Lord, and being evil expounders of what was well spoken. For they upset many, leading them away by the pretense of knowledge from Him who constituted and ordered the universe, as if they had something higher and greater to show them than the God who made the heaven and the earth and all that is in them. By skillful language they artfully attract the simple-minded into their kind of inquiry, and then crudely destroy them by working up their blasphemous and impious view about the Demiurge. Nor can their simple hearers distinguish the lie from the truth" (*CCEL; ECF;* ibid.).

In his day Irenaeus had to confront the witchery of Marcus the magician, who was deceiving many [especially the women; i.e., the silly uninformed women (see 2 Tim. 3: 6-7)]. Marcus was a false prophet that was *so called* empowering the people to prophesy (what I call prophet-lying; please see chapter four for more on this subject called "*prophet-lying*"); he also would sexually seduce the women, as well as greatly profiting financially, with his deceptive magic. This is why Irenaeus was so adamant about the saints staying in the unity of the faith and not be drawn away by this witchery or the tricks of demonic powers.

:: Closing Statement

After reading all of this it appears that the apostasy was inevitable to the apostles and bishops. In first century Christianity we see Paul constantly warning the people about the latter days, as well as the Apostle John's admonitions to the assemblies which included his great revelation disclosed to him from the Lord Jesus [Himself]. Paul stated that we who are Christians should not receive any instructions from any human being stating that the "Day of the Lord" has already come, as if it were a thing of the past. However, he stated that one thing is evident, before the Lord's return apostasy will rise *within* the *Assemblies*—for "some will depart from the faith" and then the "son of doom" will be disclosed for all to see (2Thessalonians 2:1-3; 1Timothy 4:1; Revelation 13). There is one thing that has not been made clear to us (today's Christian assemblies), which we as leaders fail to teach the people [I don't know if it is because of ignorance or we just don't care about this], but the apostles were very concerned that after their deaths that the Congregations would be devastated without apostolic authority to oversee them. The bishops that were ordained by them understood that it was the apostles desire to pass on the apostleship, but this did not take place because Ignatius and the 2nd century bishops felt that they were not apostles—so they humbled themselves to Jesus and their predecessors' authority only.

Ignatius led the charge at the close of his life to change the order of leadership to respect the apostolic office as sacred to the apostles only, because they were handpicked by Jesus. He told the people to follow their appointed Bishop, Elders and Deacons to sustain unity in the faith and to trust their Bishop as they would trust Christ. I don't believe that he said this to put men on pedestals (hierarchy) as if they are "God Almighty" [this was not his intent].

He thought to avoid heresy and apostasy that the congregations needed to stay close to leadership because the leadership would fall in line with Jesus' Messianic Authority; Jesus selected His apostles; the Apostles ordained the bishops, therefore, the Bishops have the authority from the Apostles to oversee the Assemblies, feeding the flock of God (teaching them the truth by example) and protecting them from heresies. Today's manmade embellishments and interpolations have taken over God's truths. People have no respect for the order of leadership like the early Christian fathers. I will cover more on this in chapter five when we discuss the subject; "Church Leaders are overly concerned about ministry titles."

Degeneration is plainly seen in our day, there is no doubt. Scruples are decreasing daily and some Christians are afraid to say that Jesus is the way to salvation because pantheism is on the raise (belief that all is God). Morality is becoming a thing of the past. The *so called* Church and Governments as well, are accepting the things which are antagonist against the will of God.

Thus, they think that the Bible cannot address our world's problems today, and that the Bible is outdated... "This is the 21st century and we can do what we want to do (so they believe)." The people have forgotten their God, and they are now giving in to the teachings of modern day heretics and pagan beliefs, causing apostasy to gain momentum.

Chapter Two

The Acceleration
of
Non Religion
In America:
How Will It Affect the World?

There was a study called "The American Religious Identification Survey" that was taken by Trinity College [which is located in Hartford, Connecticut]—it is so revealing when it comes to "Non-Religion" in the United States. They disclosed in 1990 that the U.S. contained only 8% of its population who considered themselves non-religions or "nones" as they like to call themselves. Eighteen years later in 2008 another TARIS survey was taken by Trinity College and the result were shocking. The "nones" have grown to 15% which has almost doubled the amount from 1990's (Survey information disclosed from U.S. News on msnbc.com website February 16, 2012).

It is now 2012 (four years later)—so roughly estimating [if they have advanced in their agenda] the "nones" should have now grown to over 16% of the population. Now this would be astonishing information! In the U.S. it is estimated that 15% of Americans are Hispanic and 13% are Black Americans; this means that the "nones" could be the largest minority group in America if their growth is sustaining its upward movement.

Why Are the People in America Leaving the So Called Churches?

There is a trend in our country as well as in the U.K. of church attendance declining steadily each year. One can travel throughout the United States and see that people are getting feed-up with ministers begging for money and the gospel is either watered down or the church organizations are making their agendas priority over the Word of God. People leaving is a sign of many falling from the faith (see chapter one on Apostasy and Degeneration).

To fill their void of church assembling, many are using sports as their new venue. Going to games and watching them on television as a way to replace their desire for God [because of church burn-out]. However, others have become workaholics. They work seven days a week from eight to sixteen hours a day, stating that they have got to pay the bills, "don't have time for church anyway, all that preacher want is your money." Then there are others who become non-religious because they have a lot of personal problems, issues and needs and the church is not helping them to get their needs met. So they result to violence and doing illegal things instead of seeking God. Furthermore, there are those who are church hopping due to dissatisfaction with various church groups because they are so dispirited and discouraged with the present church establishment and all of the pressures and demands that church leadership put on people to participate as active members of their assemblies— many eventually just give-up and become worldly due to being disgruntled with the leadership.

Finally, there are those who have totally given-up on God because the *so-called* church has hurt them and in many cases has ruined their lives. How can this be? There are many reasons for this, when we look back at the close of the first and second century of Christian history we see that the apostles and the bishops that were appointed by the apostles had all died off. Therefore, when third century Christianity began moving into the future many manmade embellish fictions began to move past the imperative Word of God. These human additions or interpolations became a seed that would grow into a large tree of schisms and deterioration of unity within the Christian congregations by which Jesus, the apostles and bishops guarded against and gave their live for.

So today the *so-called church* has gotten so far away from what the Lord and the apostles taught that these divisions have ruined them. Church leaders have put their fictional embellished clichés over the Bible and its original intentions. As the ways of humankind increased within the congregations, Satan saw the energy of the flesh at work and then much sinful behavior began to creep into the now *so- called* church. People are getting hurt by the church because the church is worldly, and does not oppose carnality, nor emphasize a godly consecrated lifestyle, that is in harmony with what Jesus and the apostles taught (John 17: 14-21).

The Apostle Peter in A.D. 67, made this statement concerning the godly prerequisites established by the power of God that is suited for the Christian lifestyle:

> *"For His divine power has bestowed upon us all things that [are requisite and suited] to life and godliness, through the [full, personal] knowledge of Him Who called us by and to His own glory and excellence (virtue). By means of these He has bestowed on us His precious and exceedingly great promises, so that through them you may escape [by flight] from the moral decay (rottenness and corruption) that is in the world because of covetousness (lust and greed), and become sharers (partakers) of the divine nature"* (2 Peter 1:3-4; Amp).

Earlier in A.D. 61, the Apostles Paul gives this explicative admonition to the assembly at Colossae:

> *"If then you have died with Christ to material ways of looking at things and have escaped from the world's crude and elemental notions and teachings of externalism, why do you live as if you still belong to the world? [Why do you submit to rules and regulations?—such as] Do not handle [this], Do not taste [that], Do not even touch [them], Referring to things all of which perish with being used. To do this is to follow human precepts and doctrines. Such [practices] have indeed the outward appearance [that popularly passes] for wisdom, in promoting self-imposed rigor of devotion and delight in self-humiliation and severity of discipline of the body, but they are of no value in checking the indulgence of the flesh (the lower nature). [Instead, they do not honor God but serve only to indulge the flesh.]"*
> (Colossians 2: 20ff; Amp; cf. Col. 3:1-10)

From medieval Christianity until now, church leaders have allowed unfair nepotism (favoritism) for friends and family members, as well as living debauchee life styles and allowing voluptuous sexual sins to be acceptable within the leadership. However, to the congregation they would not condone this type of behavior [stating: "it is sin"] but privately they would engage in these sexual sins using some of the same people who are in the congregation, telling them to not tell anyone what they are doing. Therefore, because of modern day technology and the increase of worldwide communication (radio, television, internet, smart phones, etc…) the covered-up sins are now being revealed on Catholics, Protestants, Non-denominations and Inter-denominations at a rapid pace.

These so-called church leaders are using drugs, getting drunk with alcohol and getting arrested for DUI, closet and openly *so- called gay* (sodomites and lesbians), pedophiles, addicted to pornography, adulterers, fornicators and swindlers who are after financial gain. This kind of behavior is confusion and every evil work that has raised its ugly head in this hour of degeneration to move Christians further into apostasy. If this trend continues the world will be impacted greatly, because this dwindling fear of the Lord will produce a raise in paganism, secularism, humanism and pantheism.

We Must Not Allow Sin to Win—
the World Needs God's People

Jesus said this about His followers:

> *"You are the salt of the earth, but if salt has lost its taste (its strength, its quality), how can its saltness be restored? It is not good for anything any longer but to be thrown out and trodden underfoot by men"* (Matt. 5:13; Amp).

We see here that Jesus is likening His people unto "*salt*." We humans love good seasoned foods when we indulge our favorite dishes. God speaks to us in this scripture in a way in which we can relate. Salt is normally the base for most seasoned foods. Now, what if the salt has lost its flavor of saltiness? Would it not be worthless to us? Yes, it would be worthless and we would have no use for it—it would be discarded immediately without hesitation. Therefore, the quality of the salt has diminished and is now no good for food anymore; thus, it *must* be thrown away to the dust of the earth, because of its *futility*.

It is the strength of the Christians that is sustaining the earth and that strength is Christ [the saltiness or flavor of the salt] in those who believe; for He is our only hope of glory (Col. 1:27). If we do away with Jesus and all He has instructed through His apostles, then we will become futile and non-prolific, and the world will be taken over by degenerates who are in total opposition against the teachings of Christ. All hope would be lost and no one would be saved from the wrath that is to come on the earth (Rev. 6:17; 11:18).

"But thanks [be] to God," Who has overcome the *world* (Satan's world system) through Jesus Christ; and salvation is won through His shed blood for all who believe in His name (1 Corinthians15:57; 2 Corinthians 2:14). When we believe in Christ we put our trust in the saltiness of the salt that is able to sustain us and the world. Salt is a preservative and it is used to cure meats as well. In his article called "Meat Curing" Extension Animal Food Specialist, Mr. Fredrick K.

Ray gives confirmation about salts ability to preserve, curing and its flavoring significance:

> *"Salt is the primary ingredient used in meat curing. Originally it served as a preservative by dehydration and osmotic pressure which inhibits bacterial growth. Salt still functions as a preservative in the "country style" cured meat product. The main function of salt in other cured products is to add flavor. However; even at low concentrations salt has some preservative action. Salt levels are dependent on consumer's taste, but a two to three percent concentration in the product is about right."*
> [http://pods.dasnr.okstate.edu/docushare/dsweb/ Get/Document-2055/ANSI-3994web.pdf]

When I was a boy growing up in Memphis, Tennessee I would spend some of my summer vacation with my great uncle, Preston Joyner (whom we called "Uncle Pres") and his wife Joanna. They lived in a small country town called Rossville, Tennessee, however their home was way back in the country were there was only dirt and gravel roads. They had a three room shack that sat on stones with no running water, no bathroom, no electricity and no modern day appliances except a battery operated transistor radio to hear the world news twice daily. Aunt Joanna [however, we called her "Aint Joanna"] cooked the best country ham, sausages and bacon a person could ever eat.

One summer [which was the last summer I spent with them] I witnessed my great uncle and his wife slaughter and butcher a very large hog. Uncle Pres took his rifle and shot the hog right between the eyes. My great uncle was about 98 years old at that time and he still was very good at shooting a rifle [*"a cracked shot"* was the slang we used in those days). After the slaughter, the hog was place in a wheel barrel and was carried to a large tree to be tied-up with rope, to hang upside down to clean out all of it organs which was used to assist in sausage making and the intestines for the Old Southern favorite dish call "Chitterlings."

I noticed that in my great aunts kitchen next to the large wood burning stove that there was a door to the right. One day she opened that door to show my dad their meat storage. Now, as I said earlier, they did not have electricity so they could not refrigerate the meat to preserve it from harmful bacteria growth (microorganisms). Therefore, they packed the meat with salt to cure or preserve it. I was so amazed at what I saw, and then, I heard my great aunt say to my dad, "We are going to have some good ham." I realized then that I had been eating from this stock of meat hanging on hooks in this unrefrigerated storeroom.

When I looked at these pig/hog-hides on the hooks, I could see were mold and mildew (discoloration) was trying to spread on the hides but the heavily backed salt would prevented it from growing much, which caused the hides to be sustained for eating. This was remarkable to me and at that time I was about fourteen years old, therefore until this day I will never forget what I saw that day in the summer of 1972.

I can truly say now that I clearly understand what Jesus meant when He stated Matthew 5:13 to His disciples, that "You are the salt of the earth." The pig/hog-hides represent the earth and its inhabitation and the mold and discoloration on the hides represent sin and all that is antagonistic against the will and purposes of God—and it is the packs of *Salt* (the saints or Christians) who are preventing raging sin from total consuming the world. Furthermore, if Christians fall away and renounce their faith in Jesus then this will cause sin to increase on the earth, or in other words, the saltiness leaving the salt causing the salt to become futile (worthless) and unproductive, therefore God will have no more use for it.

This is why I am sounding the alarm for all Christians everywhere to seek God with a due-diligence (like investors protecting their assets). To do an internal audit of our lives protecting God's biggest asset, namely—"The Assembly of the Upright." God needs His people to carry out His will in the earth, but if the Body of Christ has forgotten its Head then the Christians will be lost and sin will have the hour as well as the world and all that dwell within it. It is sad to me that apostasy is rising, but one thing is evident Jesus is soon to return and then all will be restore to everyone that believe in Him. Paul admonished the assembly at Thessalonica:

> *"Let no one deceive or beguile you in any way, for that day will not come except the apostasy comes*

first [unless the predicted great falling away of those who have professed to be Christians has come], and the man of lawlessness (sin) is revealed, who is the son of doom (of perdition), who opposes and exalts himself so proudly and insolently against and over all that is called God or that is worshiped, [even to his actually] taking his seat in the temple of God, proclaiming that he himself is God" (2 Thessalonica 2: 6-4; Amp).

But Paul goes on to say this to them with full assurance:

"And then the lawless one (the antichrist) will be revealed and the Lord Jesus will slay him with the breath of His mouth and bring him to an end by His appearing at His coming" (2 Thessalonica 2: 8; Amp).

After reading these words, from this man of God, I am deeply moved and feeling a little melancholy. I know that the end must come, but to see the Christian Congregations in a state of apostasy is not comforting. And I know that it was not easy for Paul to say these things because people are so bold to reject the true anomalistic Word of God. People are quick to make every excuse and not accept the fact that many are leaving the *so-called* church and the world is changing for the worst as well as the signs of the end-time are increasing for the Lord's return (Matthew 24: 3-34). Take note to what Luke said in his version in chapter twenty-one verse eleven, does this statement envision our modern times?

> *"There will be mighty and violent earthquakes, and in various places famines and pestilences (plagues: malignant and contagious or infectious epidemic diseases which are deadly and devastating); and there will be sights of terror and great signs from heaven"* (Amp).

I must say "yes" to this question. I beseech you O' people who love Jesus, let us take inventory of our lives and put away our idols and seek God's instructions which are presented in the Bible [read Joshua's plea and admonition to Israel at the close of his life; Joshua 24: 1- 29], resisting (standing firm), refusing to give in to the false prophets (preachers) of our day (Eph. 6:11-18). Editor and Presbyterian Pastor, Dr. James Russell Miller (1840-1912) made this emotional and powerful statement on Joshua 24:20 concerning idols:

> *"Anything which we keep in our hearts in the place which God ought to have is an idol, whether it be an image of wood or stone or gold, or whether it be money, or desire for fame, or love of pleasure, or some secret sin which we will not give up. If God does not really occupy the highest place in our hearts, controlling all, something else does, and that something else is an idol (J. R. Miller, Devotional Hours with the Bible)."* [http://www.

biblegateway.com/passage/?search=oshua%20
24&version=AMP]

If there has ever been a time to get our lives in line with the word of God, now is that time. Let us take an urgent heed to Dr. Miller's admonition and allow God to be in that pinnacle place of our hearts. Let us be steadfast in the faith and not be the one who is falling away from Jesus, but everyday falling even more in love with Him. **<u>We must not let sin win!</u>**

:: Closing Statement

Isn't it amazing that in this hour of degeneration we see news headlines disclosing:

"The Rise of Atheism in America"

"Episcopalians Move Closer to Allow Transgender Ministers"

"Bishop accused of Pedophilia"

"Mega-Church Pastor is Closet Homosexual"

"TV Evangelist arrested for DUI"

I know that many of you reading this book can add even more news headlines to this list that are disgusting as well. This causes the word of God to be of non-effect, and increases the opportunity for the advancement of apostasy. People are confused and they just don't know what to do. The world is saying that it is okay to be gay (sodomites and lesbians). The so-called church leaders are saying it is okay as well—to be *homosexual*. The Bible tells us that it is not okay, but many of the so-called church leaders like to say that "Jesus loves them (the gays) and we should too. How many of you have not sinned? You can't judge them. Jesus wants us to love one another and not judge people and be homophobic."

This is the rise or escalation of the degenerates, bringing a spirit of confusion, by which Satan is the author; this is not of God (1 Corinthians 14:33). The *so-called* churches of our day are accepting sodomites and lesbians because many of the mega church organizations have homosexuals leading their assemblies. Therefore, money and security is the motivation behind their sinful acts. What is basically happening to the *so-called* church is that humanism (secularism) is slowly taking over. How can this be?

Let's take a look at the meaning of the word *Humanism and it extensive stance on life.* Humanism attracts atheists, deists, naturalists, new age thinkers, freewill thinkers, environmentalists, skeptical scientists, rationalists and secularists. As one can see, humanism covers a lot of disciplines that have mutual interest. However, these disciplines are anti-God, anti-Christ and anti-supernatural. Humans are in control of their own lives and are void of supernatural intervention. In other words humanity is all that matters, believing in a God of providence is just superstition—he does not exist to assist humanity. Therefore, it is only the philosophies of men (*secular humanism*) that matters, not the Bible or any religiosity.

The philosophies of men are taking over the *so-called* church with a gradual approach—osmotically absorbing over time until God's words becomes irrelevant in its meaning and human words become relevant over and above the Word of God. Thus, with the rise of non-religion in our world moving at its present pace, I am afraid that we are going to see secular humanism strengthened in our day. This is bad news because there are so many disgruntled Christians who will be vulnerable to this movement. We are already seeing the pantheistic environmental movement making big strides in Christendom within the 21st century, with their "Green Bible" which is endorsed by two secular groups: The Sierra Club and The Humane Society.

We as Christians must not lose our focus [which is Christ Jesus]. He is our main emphasis and not the cares of this world and human intellectualism. We must come together in unity and remove all the schisms, splits and divisions and deliver the pure unadulterated Word of God that is the absolute truth and not humanism. Finally, Paul's statement to the assembly at Colossae is precisely the truth, when he cited:

> *"See to it that no one carries you off as spoil or makes you yourselves captive by his so-called philosophy and intellectualism and vain deceit*

(idle fancies and plain nonsense), following human tradition (men's ideas of the material rather than the spiritual world), just crude notions following the rudimentary and elemental teachings of the universe and disregarding [the teachings of] Christ (the Messiah)" (Col. 2:8; Amp).

Chapter Three

Disrespect and Insolence
Are
Increasing Against the Church
In Our Contemporary Times

Many in Christendom (especially in the United States) would blame the Devil and say that the Church is starting to experience persecution because the Government has turned their back on Jesus and the Gospel. This statement has some merit, but it is not the whole truth. Most of the problems lie within the *so-called* Church itself, due to the raise in hypocrisy as was mentioned in my closing statement in chapter two. However, in this chapter we will be discussing insolence against the Church and how the Church is becoming more secular in their make-up and the spirit of the anti-Christ is growing in the world, because the *so-called* Church has failed to represent true holiness and faith towards God.

Paul the apostle was very clear to Titus (his son in the Gospel) about holy living when he stated:

> *"For the grace of God (His unmerited favor and blessing) has come forward (appeared) for the deliverance from sin and the eternal salvation for all mankind. It has trained us to reject and renounce all ungodliness (irreligion) and worldly (passionate) desires, to live discreet (temperate, self-controlled), upright, devout (spiritually whole) lives in this present world, Awaiting and looking for the [fulfillment, the realization of our] blessed hope, even the glorious appearing of our great God and Savior Christ Jesus (the Messiah, the Anointed One), Who gave Himself on our behalf that He might redeem us (purchase our freedom) from all iniquity and purify for Himself a people [to be peculiarly His own, people who are] eager and enthusiastic about [living a life that is good and filled with] beneficial deeds"* (Titus 2:11-14; Amp).

God's grace has delivered us if we believe in His Word. The problem we have, is that there is way too much lip service and not enough doers of the word [as James admonished the twelve Hebrew tribes of Diaspora (James 1:22-23)]. We are not turning away from evil and repudiating sin like Paul instructed us by which the grace of God has equipped the saints. Instead, on the contrary, we are sinful and we have allowed evil to enter our assemblies. Witchcraft is prevalent in the *so-called* churches and no one can spot it because the people can't discern evil from good.

This is a serious problem, the prophet Isaiah said:

> *"Woe to those who call evil good and good evil, who put darkness for light and light for darkness, who put bitter for sweet and sweet for bitter"* (Isa. 5:20; Amp)!

Are we so drunk in our folly that we are allowing secularism to take over our congregations? The working of the flesh is taking center stage among our people and the leaders cannot discern this because evil has become good and good has become evil. For example: Do you think that Jesus would approve of His assemblies participating in Halloween activities (celebrating death and the spirits of darkness). Many would like to say that "this is for the children"—"we are not serious"—"we are just having fun!" It is a shame that in the name of children we justify witchery disguised as a "Fall Festival." It appears that there is no difference between the *so-called* church and the world. Whatever the world is doing the *so-called* church is following suit. Jesus cased out devils and tormented the spirits of darkness with His presence. Christians are to be children of light and not darkness. We are to have the sweet aroma of the Lord on us [liken unto the smell of beautiful flowers] and not the stench of hell and demons [which are likened unto the smell of sulfur].

So why is the world disrespecting the *so-called* Church? No one, absolutely no one in this world likes a hypocrite. The world sees a *so-called* Church that is not Christ-like, so they become insolent to those who say that they are Christians, because they see no true devotion. The same people partying in the clubs, drinking in the bars, getting high on drugs and participating in all kinds of sexual vices are calling themselves Christians. Saying that God loves them and that they can always repent of their sins—He knows that the flesh is weak.

No wonder people are angry with the *so-called church*! The people need a place to turn to when they are tired of their sinful lifestyles, and they can't find that place in the *so-called church*, so they go to paganism, pantheism or the occult for some kind of spiritual satisfaction. Where is the enthusiasm for godliness? The world can't see it in the *so-called Church,* because the *so-called* Church is not serious about their Christian convictions—there is no passion or godly enthusiasm. Back in 1969 and in the early 1970's jazz musicians Les McCann and Eddie Harris made a statement in a song that should stir the *so-called* Christians to get their lives in order and stop all the hypocrisies. I think that these lyrics are a cry to God for help because they could not see God in the *so-called church*. Here is the excerpt or the part in the song where Les McCann makes this salient point:

"Church on Sunday, sleep and nod
Tryin' to duck, the wrath of God
Preacher's fillin' us with pride
They all tryin' a-teach us
What they think is right
They really got to be some kind of nut!
I can't use it!

Tryin' to make it real compared to what"

(http://www.smartlyrics.com/Song606746-Les-McCann--
Eddie-Harris-Compared-To-What-lyrics.aspx)

Later in the song he asked the question *"A-Where's my God"* (ibid)? The cry is that these men are discouraged and they feel like many others, that there is no were to turn, because they cannot see God in the *so-called* Church. Therefore, if there is no God in the people then there must not be a God at all. We as people of God must change this perception, and we must change it now!

What Can We Do?

I have found that over the years that the best critics of the *so-called* Church are those common everyday people who tell it like it is [they have no reason to lie]. Their argument is that they don't go to church [per se] because the people are a bunch of *hypocrites.* Years ago living in Enid, Oklahoma we were out witnessing to lost sinners (you know, people that are not active or involved in a *so-called* church). I was standing across the street in front of the local Pub/Club near a storefront area and a very tough looking young man [with a chip on his shoulder (sort of speak)] was sitting on the concreted area at the storefront with a tall can of beer in his hand setting it down and picking it up. He look at me and said [and I quote]: "Hey, let me tell you something, those same people that go to that church down the street, when they get out, they come right down here with me and go to the club and drink a brew (beer)." I said to him, "Hey man, you live right; you do what is right; you live for God." Then he dropped his head turning it side to side saying to me, "Man your right—your right."

There are several things we can do as Christians that the apostle Paul has already instructed us to do in Titus 2:11-14:

1. **We Must Take Heed to God's Grace-** Even though we corrupted sinners do not deserve the blessings of God, He has come to deliver us because His love is ineffable. God hates sin, so He sent Jesus to deliver all humans from eternal perdition [if they believe (John 3:16-17)]. Therefore, we must acknowledge the final Spotless Lamb oblation and propitiations for sin which God has accepted through His Son.

2. **The Grace of God "Has Trained Us to Reject and Renounce" All that is Antagonistic to the Will and Purposes of God-** What is God's will and purpose? His will and purpose is to oppose sin and degradation. God's Grace is our teacher and He has taught us that we

should not serve sin (Romans 6). We are not to choose the lower life of ungodliness and fleshly desires, because if we do, we will be fulfilling the lust of the flesh (please read Ephesians 2:1-9), which would cause humanity to not see the light of God in our lives. Jesus said: *"Let your light so shine before men that they may see your moral excellence and your praiseworthy, noble, and good deeds and recognize and honor and praise and glorify your Father Who is in heaven"* (Matt. 5:16; Amp). It is the lust of the flesh, the lust of the eyes and the pride of life (1 John 2:16) that is destroying the *so-called* Church. Therefore, we are enticed to sin against God because we want to be worldly, not because anyone is making or forcing us to do anything—we have no self-control—we are weak, pathetic and selfish. Thus the fruit of the Spirit must be seen—not the workings of the flesh (Galatians 5: 19ff).

3. **We Must Live a Life of Temperance, Self-Discipline and Self-Control**- A true Christians must have a strong mind and will to accept godliness and pursue righteousness. We must show resilience and toughness in the faith to withstand worldly temptations. If we give in to the world, then the world can't see God in us, which means we have failed God by not producing enough light to a dark world. Jesus said that *"Ye are the light of the world"* (Matt. 5:14; KJV). If this is the case then we should be doing all we can to generate light and not dim our light or let it go out.

4. **We Must be Devoted to Righteousness**- We as true believers in Christ must be dedicated and consistent

in the faith; living committed lives of decency, morals, virtue and scruples. God's spiritual rectitude is the way of the straight and the strait & narrow—it is the Way of Truth and Life (Matt. 7:14; John 14:6).

5. **We Must be Enthusiastic About Godly Living**- We are to be excited about our future; that someday we will be in the Lord's presence [forever to be with Him (2 Cor. 5:8-9)], and godly living is our joy because we know if we continue in the faith that someday we will hear Jesus say, "Well done my good and faithful servant" (Matt. 25:21). If we have been "*bought with a price*" by the precious blood of Jesus (1 Cor. 6: 19-20; 7: 22-23), why are we still slaves to sin and not truly serving the Lord (Rom. 6: 5-6; 12)? A true servant of God is obedient to his Master and worships the very ground He walks on. To be called "O ye of little faith" should not be our goal. Our goal is to be pleasing in Jesus' sight by being productive children of light. In this hour of degeneration it is not time for us to throw in the towel [sort of speak], but have a fervent passion for true holiness and faith towards God, that will cause others to be ignited by our enthusiasm and eagerness to do the Lord's bidding.

Before We Can Command Respect, We Must First Earn It

In 1Timothy 4:12, Paul instructs Timothy to "*Let no one despise or think less of you because of your youth, but be an example (pattern) for the believers in speech, in conduct, in love, in faith, and in purity* (Amp). Paul made this statement to Timothy because he knew how important it was for Timothy to earn the respect of the people. So, how does one earn the respect of the people? In order to do this, your lifestyle must be an example of godliness, true holiness and faith in Jesus Christ.

If Timothy can't lead by example then he will not gain any respect from the people nor can he demand people to respect him—his leadership abilities would be a total absolute turn-off to the assembly. As we can see Timothy is young and the elders are watching him to see if he will fall into temptation. If he maintains his walk with God then they will respect him and honor his words, because they know that he is serious about the Lord's work and the people of God's well being. Seriousness is what's lacking in the *so-called* Church today. Where are the solemnity, sincerity, honesty, earnestness and genuineness of God's people?

✹ Demanding Respect Is Not an Option

How can the contemporary *so-called* Church demand respect when their lifestyles are not conducive to true holiness and righteous living? If Christians are the *salt of the earth*, one of the definitions of this statement is that God has given His authority to His people to represent Him on the earth; to resist evil [not indulge in it] and overcome every form of wickedness that would hinder the advancement of the Gospel and faith towards God—remember, salt is a preservative. We must walk in God's authority with a commanding impression by which people will automatically see God in His people and say, "What must I do to be saved?"[Acts 2: 37-38] Our lives are to mirror Christ! That is why at Antioch, Syria the believers were first called Christians because their lives reflected Jesus' authority (see Acts 11: 19-26).

The Spirit of Anti-Christ

The spirit of anti-Christ in our day is covered under the blanket of humanism, secularism and pantheism. The Church [so-called] is allowing the degenerates to take the lead in the congregations of the assemblies. Our concern is no longer what the Bible teaches (when it comes to the subject of what is right or wrong)—instead we only are concerned about political correctness and humanity's opinions over God's truths. The apostles in their day mostly had to deal with *Gnostic Docetism* [Jesus did not come in the flesh or have a human body—it only appears that he died on the cross—it was just a magical illusion].

However, on the other hand today those who truly fear the Lord have to deal with sodomites (effeminate men), lesbians (women trying to be virile) and same-sex marriage, as being okay, because Jesus loves everyone, regardless of their sexual orientation. Even though the Holy Bible speaks out against these abominations [likening this to lying with strange flesh as mentioned in Jude 1: 6-8 referring to angels lying with woman and the "unnatural" vices of Sodom and Gomorrah and their "sensual" perversities (see further abominations in Deuteronomy 22: 5; Leviticus 18: 22-23; 1 Corinthians 6:9)]. Every time we see this kind of sin in the Bible mentioned—death and destruction is not far away:

I. Sodom and Gomorrah—most of the Vale of Siddim destroyed (Genesis 19: 1-29).
II. The Tribe of Benjamin almost completely wiped-out (Judges 19ff)
III. Paul states that those who do such acts deserve death (Romans 1: 18ff).

The spirit of anti-Christ is very subtle and shrewd in our modern times. Many are being deceived and don't care or just don't realize what is happening to them. Witchcraft and magic are also tools that the spirit of anti-christ is using to infiltrate the *so-called* churches; causing apostasy as well as undetected false prophets who speak foolishness like, "prophesy to yourselves" (we will speak more on this subject in chapter four of this book).

:: In Summation

Insolence is increasing against the *so-called* Church because the churches are allowing the way of humanism and secular political correctness to take the lead in their assemblies. It appears that the *so-called* churches in our modern times are demanding respect instead of commanding respect [which means we must be a *living* example of godliness in the earth]. No one likes a hypocrite, and in this hour of degeneration the *so-called* Church is saying one thing and is doing another, therefore the people are confused and they are just not sure if there is a *"God"* because they can't see God in His people. This chapter is a wake-up call for all Christians everywhere to go to the word of God and take God at His Word. For far too long we have been taking the words of mankind and humanism over the Bible. We must resist the sexual sins and witchery that are leading many to apostasy, in this degenerated hour. We are to be the light of the world and the salt of the earth as Jesus analogized (Matt. 5: 13-16). We are not to be a part of the problems, but we are to be a part of the solutions, for people to experience the *Blessed Hope that is in Christ Jesus.*

Chapter Four

The Rise of Prophet-lying Or False Prophecy in this Hour of Degeneration

"*For this is a rebellious people, faithless and lying sons, children who will not hear the law and instruction of the Lord; Who [virtually] say to the seers [by their conduct], See not! And to the prophets, Prophesy not to us what is right! Speak to us smooth things, prophesy deceitful illusions*" (Isaiah 30: 9-10; Amp).

Before I get to the gist of my subject "Prophet-lying"—I want to bring to your attention 1Kings 13:1-32. These verses of scripture are one of the best examples of prophet-lying. Prophet-lying can be very detrimental—it can even get a person killed—you must read these verses through its entirety to get the complete narrative. These passages of biblical scriptures will prove to the reader that lying prophecies are dangerous. Jesus said this about prophet-lying, in Matthew 24:11; "And many false prophets will rise up and deceive *and* lead many into error (Amp). Please open your Bible at this time to Ezekiel chapter 13 and read what the Lord said through His prophet about prophet-lying and lying divinations.

It is amazing to me that in these times in which we live, that humans are so vulnerable to false prophesies or as I call it "prophet-lying." There are many in our world today that practices this art of deception—speaking over people with words of prophesies that never come to pass. Telling people that God is going to prosper them and give them a new job or make them rich—as well as making general generic (nonspecific) statements that have no significance or substance whatsoever.

These are worthless, futile, imprecise, and inaccurate statements of the flesh that are not spiritual discerned or divinely inspired, but comes from the heart of the person giving a so-called ***word*** to an individual. When these statements are made the person giving the so-called *word* say to everyone that is present that they can claim another person's word for themselves if they desire—therefore many use the cliché, "I receive it" or "I receive that." None of this foolish nonsense is written in God's word as His instructions for the saints (the people of God). This is modern day poppycock that is incongruent (inappropriate)—it is the workings of the flesh—witchcraft; sorcery (Galatians 5: 19-21).

False prophesy

The true prophet of God, "Jeremiah" prophesied destruction to Judah (the Southern Kingdom—with emphasis on *Jerusalem*) because of their sin (c.f. Samuel's prophesy to Israel; 1 Sam. 12: 14-25), but the false prophets opposed the word of the Lord and Jeremiah prophesied these words that had come to pass by 586 B.C.

> *"Then the Lord said to me, The [false] prophets prophesy lies in My name. I sent them not, neither have I commanded them, nor have I spoken to them. They prophesy to you a false or pretended vision, a worthless divination [conjuring or practicing magic, trying to call forth the responses supposed to be given by idols], and the deceit of their own minds. Therefore thus says the Lord concerning the [false] prophets who prophesy in My name— although I did not send them—and who say, Sword and famine shall not be in this land: By sword and famine shall those prophets be consumed. And the people to whom they prophesy shall be cast out in the streets of Jerusalem, victims of famine and sword;*

*and they shall have none to bury them—them,
their wives, their sons, and their daughters. For I
will pour out their wickedness upon them [and not
on their false teachers only, for the people could not
have been deceived except by their own consent]"*
(Jer. 14: 1-16: Amp; cf. Jer. 23: 9ff).

One thing we must remember when dealing with
prophecy. *The result of the prophecy or its fulfillment must
equate with the statement of the prophecy given (italic emphasis
added)*—and Jeremiah's prophecy did just that. In B.C.
586 Jerusalem was invaded and destroyed by Babylon
and placed under king Nebuchadnezzar's great power and
authority. If the prophecy given does not produce exactly
what is stated, then the prophecy is false or **the prophet
has lied**. Jeremiah's prophecy is purely the word of God and
he delivered a word in season that confirmed his prophetic
predecessors and their prognostications against the sins of
Judah and Israel.

During the times of Isaiah the prophet, in B.C. 722,
king Sargon II of Assyria seized Samaria and captured the
ten tribes of Israel, ending the Northern Kingdom. One
would think that Judah would have learned from Israel's
defiant antagonism against the will of God, but they did
not and destruction came to them as well some 136 years
later [approximately].

Let's look at another example of prophet-lying which
occurred when Ahab was king of Israel and Jehoshaphat
was king of Judah, around 853 B.C. This would be the last

year of Ahab's life on earth because Elijah the prophet of God had prognosticated the doom and demise of Ahab, due to him coveting Naboth the Jezreelite's vineyard that was near the King's Place. He wanted to buy it from him, but Naboth did not want to sell because the vineyard was part of his inheritance. Therefore, Ahab's controlling wife Jezebel, wrote a decree to kill Naboth [in the name of the king] for not selling his vineyard to him, Ahab would later loose his life due to prophet-lying (Please read 1 Kings 21 in its entirety).

In 1 Kings 22: 1-40 we see a classic example of the result of the prophecy or its fulfillment actually equating with the statement of the prophecy given. Thus we pick-up the scene in vv. 3-4 with Ahab asking Jehoshaphat to go up with him into battle against the Syrians to gain possession of Ramoth in Gilead even though there had been peace between the two nations for three years. Of course Jehoshaphat agreed with him and would oblige his offer, but first, because King Jehoshaphat was a godly man and respected the Word of the LORD—he asked King Ahab if there was any word from God on this immediate venture into harms way?

After the king of Judah's request for a word from the LORD; Ahab rounded up 400 prophets who all acquiesced that God said to them that He has given the Syrians into the hands of the King of Israel. However, this was not enough for Jehoshaphat [which I thought was quite remarkable; most people after hearing from 400 people all saying the same thing at the same time would have been convinced that all would be well]. But like I said earlier King Jehoshaphat was a godly man and he wanted to be sure that this was the will of God.

The Great Prophet Micaiah—A True Prophet of God

Nevertheless, Jehoshaphat inquired that King Ahab would bring forth another prophet besides these agreeable ones because there could be more to this then what has been stated [*this is superlative wisdom in its greatest hour by King Jehoshaphat*]. Therefore Ahab requested that Micaiah be brought before him and the king of Judah. Before he was brought to the two kings, Micaiah was warned by the messenger to consent (or go alone with the other 400 prophets) and not foul things up. There is one thing sure about Micaiah; he was a man that was confident in what God would tell him and there is no way that he would follow the will of man no matter how hard he tried—he just could not do it.

Now Ahab did not like Micaiah because he always would prophecy the truth, and as many of us know the truth can hurt you if you are living a wicked lifestyle like King Ahab was living. As we can see when reading this text that Ahab had no spiritual discernment or unction from the Holy One. Therefore, he would call godliness evil because he could not discern right from wrong or good from evil. Micaiah tried to *prophet-lie* like the others but the King of Israel scolded him to tell the truth. However, when Ahab did that, the spirit of the Lord began to speak through His prophet Micaiah, prognosticating Ahab's demise and downfall.

Thus, we see later, that after the death of King Ahab, the prophecy of Elijah [the man of God] was fulfilled when he stated, "Thus says the Lord: In the place where dogs licked the blood of Naboth shall dogs lick your blood, even yours" (1 Kings 21: 19; Amp). God allowed a lying spirit to speak through the 400 prophets so that Ahab's reign as king of Israel would come to an end. Micaiah was the only prophet that was not counted with the 400 that was accurate in his statement.

So-called Prominent Preachers Who Prophet-lie

Just because prominent people are speaking words of prophecy to congregations, it does not indicate that it is a word from God or a word in season. I have witnessed for the past 32+ years a lot of so-called prominent preachers prophet-lying to a lot of people. Probably 95% of this deceptive art is seen mostly in Charismatic /Pentecostal settings. Even though there are a lot of true prophecies given, it appears that the false prophecies outweigh the true prophecies significantly. Telling someone that they are going to get a new job or make a lot of money is obscure and vague (it is not specific).

Telling people that God is going to heal them overtime is also a sure sign that that person is speaking from their heart and not from the spirit of God. If the person speaking prophecies of healing and the healing never manifest then the art of deception has shown its ugly head. People stuttering or stammering and pressing to try to find a word to give to people is a sure sign that they are speaking from their own heart. In this hour of degeneration many so-called preachers use this art to stir-up the emotions of the people to get them to get excited [which causes dancing, shouting and crying—in which they call themselves "*having church*" (**having church** is not written in the Bible)].

Then at the close of the so-called *service* they call for an offering to rob the people of their money, saying that they are giving into good ground when they give to this particular preacher's ministry [this is also not written in the Bible]. It is true that once you are emotionally involved with what has just taken place, you would look like a fool if you do not put some money in the offering basket. Also the same preacher that just prophet-lied to the congregation, gets-up and say that God just spoken to him/her that there are ten people in the room who can give 1,000.00 dollars, twenty people that can give 500.00 dollars and forty people that can give 250.00 dollars.

If you can't see that this is deception at its best then you are thick-headed, blind, stupid, and ignorant. Did Jesus ever do things like this or His apostles? Of course not! You can't find one scripture in the New Testament that supports this type of behavior. But on the contrary, Paul speaks to Timothy prophetically about the future—how people will accept humanities lies over God's truths:

> *"For the time is coming when [people] will not tolerate (endure) sound and wholesome instruction, but, having ears itching [for something pleasing*

*and gratifying], they will gather to themselves one
teacher after another to a considerable number,
chosen to satisfy their own liking and to foster the
errors they hold, And will turn aside from hearing
the truth and wander off into myths and manmade fictions"* (2 Tim. 4:3-4; Amp).

The Corporeal Life of Jesus Was Prophetic in Everyway

When we look at the human life of Jesus we see that
everything about Him was prophetic. The Old Testament
concealed the promised Messiah and the New Testament
revealed that Promise. In my book "His Mighty Word of
Power" I disclosed that God in His creation of the human
habitat (known as planet earth), had a redemption plan
in place for fallen humanity, because He knew that Satan
would trick them with his witchery of deception concerning
the Tree of Life and the Tree of the Knowledge of Good
and Evil (Gen. 3). He would speak to Eve with part of the
truth, speaking into existence their doom but covering it up
with intelligent words of a lying divination, or a premonition
to deceive God's true prognostication if they would obey
his word instead of God's spoken Word (Hebrew: *amar*)
(Greek: *logos*).

Jesus said these words: *"I am the Way and the Truth and
the Life; no one comes to the Father except by (through) Me"*
(John 14:6; Amp). The Tree of Life in the center of Garden
of Eden (Gen. 2:9) is a typology of the Son of God because
He is the Way to eternal life. If Adam and Eve would have

eaten from this tree they would have had life everlasting, but after eating from the tree of the Knowledge of Good and Evil they were given the death penalty (Gen 3: 22-24).

Throughout the Old and New Testament we see the true prophecies that came to past about Jesus the Messiah and there are yet still prophecies to be fulfilled; especially when it comes to the *Parousia* (the Second Advent of Christ). Zacharias' prophetic word inspired by the Holy Ghost reaches from antiquity till the birth of John the Baptist [which was three months before Jesus' birth]. His statement is the fulfilling of all Old Testament prophecies concerning the Messiah and His harbinger the prophet, John the Baptizer:

> *"Blessed (praised and extolled and thanked) be the Lord, the God of Israel, because He has come and brought deliverance and redemption to His people! And He has raised up a Horn of salvation [a mighty and valiant Helper, the Author of salvation] for us in the house of David His servant— This is as He promised by the mouth of His holy prophets from the most ancient times [in the memory of man]— That we should have deliverance and be saved from our enemies and from the hand of all who detest and pursue us with hatred; To make true and show the mercy and compassion and kindness [promised] to our forefathers and to remember and carry out His holy covenant [to bless, which is all the more sacred because it is made by God Himself], That covenant*

He sealed by oath to our forefather Abraham" (Luke 1: 68-73; Amp; see the Abrahamic Covenant [Genesis. 15]).

All the prophecies spoken about Jesus were true [and this cannot be denied]. Arguably the book of Isaiah is indeed the most prophetic of all the Old Testament books when it comes to Messianic prophesies about Jesus. I call the book of Isaiah the *solo* Gospel of the Old Testament. In chapter nine of the book of Isaiah, he prognosticates this [about the coming Messiah] with clarity and precision of speech:

> *"For to us a Child is born, to us a Son is given; and the government shall be upon His shoulder, and His name shall be called Wonderful Counselor, Mighty God, Everlasting Father [of Eternity], Prince of Peace. Of the increase of His government and of peace there shall be no end, upon the throne of David and over his kingdom, to establish it and to uphold it with justice and with righteousness from the [latter] time forth, even forevermore. The zeal of the Lord of hosts will perform this"* (vv. 6-7; Amp).

And then Jesus said this about Himself, confirming that the Old Testament secretly concealed the Messianic prophecies concerning Him:

> *"This is what I told you while I was still with you: everything which is written concerning Me in the*

Law of Moses and the Prophets and the Psalms must be fulfilled. Then He [thoroughly] opened up their minds to understand the Scriptures, And said to them, Thus it is written that the Christ (the Messiah) should suffer and on the third day rise from (among) the dead, And that repentance [with a view to and as the condition of] forgiveness of sins should be preached in His name to all nations, beginning from Jerusalem" (Luke 24: 44-47; Amp).

Thus we can see that the Bible is a prophetic book that is accurate in its prophetic delivery and fulfillments when it comes to Jesus the Messiah. When God speaks it is truth and nothing but the truth and there are no meaningless words of futility. Humanity in there fictional prophet –lying speak frivolous words of nonsense that are never questioned by those who the so-called *word* was give to. Why is this? Why are they still following these false prophets who lie to them? This is most puzzling and is a great concern.

:: Closing Statement

As I close this chapter I would like to reiterate on the definition of a true prophecy—which is: *The fulfillment of the prophecy (or its result) must equate with the statement of the prophecy given [italics emphasized].* If the person giving the prophecy delivers a *word* to another and it does not come to past, then this is proof of an unfulfilled prophecy—meaning that this individual has just spoken from his/her heart and prophet-lied. It is sad to me when I look at today's Christendom; the position of the godly prophetic seer and the gift of prophecy have been very much abused.

People are using witchcraft and psychological trickery in the name of "Thus saith, the Lord!" False prophets and false prophecies are everywhere and it appears that no one dares to point this out, and for some apparent deceptive reason people in leadership positions seem to just not care about this. However, there are some true prophecies given, but like I said earlier the false prophecies seem to outweigh the true ones and this is not good.

If we want to truly know the will of the Lord and His illuminating guidance for our lives, we must first take heed to the words of the Apostle Paul's admonition to the assembly in Ephesus:

> "*Therefore He says, Awake, O sleeper, and arise from the dead, and Christ shall shine (make day dawn) upon you and give you light. Look carefully then how you walk! Live purposefully and worthily and accurately, not as the unwise and witless, but as wise (sensible, intelligent people), Making the very most of the time [buying up each opportunity], because the days are evil. Therefore do not be vague and thoughtless and foolish, but understanding and firmly grasping what the will of the Lord is*" (Ephesians 5: 14-17; Amp).

As Paul points out we must make good use of our time, which means we must seek the Lord through Bible study and research scriptural intent instead of the manmade fictions and interpolations that have stolen the true meaning of the Holy Scriptures. This is an evil time in which we live and it is now time that we become fully aware of our surroundings and not get caught-up in worldliness, false teachings and untrue prophetic utterances that have damaged the integrity of the *so-called church* that is supposed to be in Christ Jesus.

Chapter Five

In this Hour of Degeneration The Church Leaders Are Overly Concerned About Ministry Titles

Why are ministry leaders so concerned about ministry titles and offices? This is a very important question because in today's society some Christian people actually think that Jesus left a hierarchy on earth that people should go to; as if these individuals are God or God like. The minister is placed in a position like a King or an Emperor instead of a servant [read Mark 9: 33-37]. They sit in their Cathedrals and Temples in large chairs like thrones and they are given the titles of Pope, Your Eminence, Arch Bishop, Cardinal,

Reverend, Father Divine, Apostle, Your Grace, Your Holiness, Pastor and the list goes on.

[Jesus] as He was reclining with the twelve apostles at the final Passover Seder Dinner, which He had with them, over heard His disciples argue and dispute over who would be considered supreme or most important [*the greatest in authority*]. He "*said to them, the kings of the Gentiles are deified by them and exercise lordship [ruling as emperor-gods] over them; and those in authority over them are called benefactors and well-doers. But this is not to be so with you; on the contrary, let him who is the greatest among you become like the youngest, and him who is the chief and leader like one who serves. For who is the greater, the one who reclines at table (the master), or the one who serves? Is it not the one who reclines at table? But I am in your midst as One Who serves. And you are those who have remained [throughout] and persevered with Me in My trials; And as My Father has appointed a kingdom and conferred it on Me, so do I confer on you [the privilege and decree], That you may eat and drink at My table in My kingdom and sit on thrones, judging the twelve tribes of Israel*" (Luke 22: 24-30; Amp; cf. Mark 9: 33-37).

So where did this notion of hierarchy derive from—if Jesus Himself did not teach or approve this? You notice after reading this texted that Jesus only emphasize a position of royalty after the apostles enter the Kingdom of Heaven—once they have passed through this life on earth [not before]. Therefore, His former statement emphasized beginning in a low position as one who serves [liken unto a young apprentice—but wise in their service]. In John

13: 1-15 we see Jesus washing the disciples feet (even Judas Iscariot feet—the betrayer) using a servants towel serving the disciples as one in a low position.

This was unheard of because Jesus was great in their sight—they never thought that He would do anything like this or stoop that low to wash their dirty feet. Once again (and this was the final time) Jesus is showing His disciples that as long as they are on the earth they must be servants to their fellowman—and not try to be the greatest or a big time famous preacher. The prosperity Gospel teaches that God wants to make us rich right here on earth, right now [name it and claim it, snatch it and grab it, confess it and believe it and you will receive it (*the emphasis is on materialism and earthly gain*)]—this is poppycock and based from the witchery of the Law of Manifestation which is pure pantheism.

Jesus never taught His disciple this nonsense, but on the contrary, He taught them the importance of being a servant that works towards meeting the needs of others and bringing comfort to believers [in Christ]—not having the people of God serve them as if they were kings on thrones.

As the apostles of the first century began their cessation due to martyrdom and old age—the bishops who were appointed by them would not place themselves into apostolic leadership. They respected the office of the apostles as Christ's handpicked leaders for the New Testament assemblies that were built upon the foundation of [Him] Jesus Christ by which God made the increase (1 Cor. 3: 4-11). Ignatius, Polycarp, Clement and others did not try to take on apostolic authority, because during their times all the bishops tended to their own flocks or congregational jurisdictions. They understood that apostolic leadership was gone and that Christian unity was vital to guard against apostasy.

Now, since the appointed bishops did not want to extend the apostleship, but rather tended to the needs of their flocks, why are some today saying that God has called them to be apostles? This is a good question that needs to be answered. Some would say that God has called me to be an apostle and then there are others who just feel like they are apostles. However, there are some who just want to be called apostle because they can't be ordained as a bishop in their *so-called* church organization—saying, "Bishops are appointed by men, but I am an apostle, I was appointed by God." This statement is not fully the truth, because there is once mentioned in Acts 1:20ff that God and the eleven apostles worked together to fill the vacant position once held by Judas Iscariot. The apostles selected two men as candidates for the twelfth apostolic bishopric and then they asked God, which one is His choice. Therefore after drawing lots, they elected Mathias (see Ps. 69:25; 109:8 in relation to Judas Iscariot with emphasis on Acts 1:20). Lastly there are some who just want to be a big time preacher, so they call themselves apostle.

Apostolic Pretenders

John records in Revelation 2: 1-2, Jesus commending the assembly at Ephesus for not tolerating evil men that call themselves apostles due to their evaluation and critical assessment of these men's behaviors and lifestyles. Jesus said:

> *"I know your industry and activities, laborious toil and trouble, and your patient endurance, and how you cannot tolerate wicked [men] and have tested and critically appraised those who call [themselves] apostles (special messengers of Christ) and yet are not, and have found them to be impostors and liars"* (Rev.2: 2; Amp).

Even in those days, men were going around calling themselves apostles, trying to impress the people with their unearned title. This title [apostle], Jesus only bestowed on a few people He humbled, and they felt unworthy to be called *apostle*, because they knew that they were mere men and sinful. However, it was Jesus who delivered them and granted salvation for their souls, giving them a platform to witness in His name and to build the *Ekklesia* (the assembly of the saints). That is why the early Christian Father's would not call themselves *apostles* because they knew that Jesus granted this office to only a few to begin the Christian era.

Personal Life Verses the Office Held

The title of one's office is not more important than ones ethical, moral and personal life of integrity. I often tell children that it is more important to be a good citizen then it is for one to make good grades in school. Many people may disagree with this statement because of the emphasis on academics in this world. Yes, academics are important and scholarship must be respected—I myself possess a doctorate degree.

However, what good is it for a person to be an honor student but end-up becoming an embezzler, extortioner, thief, crooked politician, gangster, whoremonger, homosexual, pedophile, and pornographer. Would that not be considered a waste of intellectual power and talent? Therefore, if one honors God with good citizenship, although they may not be the brightest students in the classroom or the smartest person in their profession—their life of integrity and ethics [with good morals values] is far more superior then the one who has the intellectual edge.

In our society today it is now common to hear about mega ministry scandals. Well known preachers with bad ethics and some committing immoral sexual sins and preaching on television with a straight face denying their accusers, but later they admit they have sinned or they do a financial settlement behind closed doors to suppress the issue that is bogging down their *so-called* ministry. When are we going to wake-up to the fact that the advancing of the Word of God in our lives is more important than the ministry offices held?

Also, you so-called clergy or ministers, where is your fear of the Lord, that you would commit such acts of disobedience and not be convicted of your sin? Thus, constantly entertaining the people with your different preaching styles and not being sincere with them or with God because you are so full of yourselves and yourself images and not full of the presence of the Lord God Who has given you life and freedom to serve Him and His flock.

You are unwise and unholy and bringing a curse upon the people because of your sinful lifestyles that you have covertly hidden (crypto-iniquity), but later, your sinful acts are revealed to the whole world. Therefore, this causes many of your followers to apostate, giving attention to seducing spirits which leads them astray with devilish doctrines (1Timothy 4:1).

:: Closing Statement with Salient Points about Sinful Humanity

There is nothing more important than ones relationship with their Maker, and to be entrusted with the Gospel ministry one should be more eager to live a life by which God would be pleased with. Yes, none of us are perfect and it is a fact that human beings are sinners. Here are some verses of scripture that support this statement:

i. *Since all have sinned and are falling short of the honor and glory which God bestows and receives.* (Romans 3:23; Amp)

It is the redemptive blood of Jesus that has declared us righteous by faith in Him, and the grace of God that has given us justification. We truly believe that we are inculpable, because Jesus died for our sins and iniquities (Romans 3:24-26; 5:8-10).

> *ii. Therefore, as sin came into the world through one man, and death as the result of sin, so death spread to all men, [no one being able to stop it or to escape its power] because all men sinned.* (Romans 5:12; Amp)

In my book "His Mighty Word of Power," I made this statement about the origin of humans sinning against God: "*God created earthborn man (male and female) without the death penalty. Nevertheless, however, it was sin (Satan) that enticed mankind to disobey God's law, leading to a death penalty for all human beings" (Genesis 3).* [Chapter 3 "Yom" Genesis 1:3ff; p.25, *HMWP—TPJ*] Adam being a type of the Son of God [as well as being the first son of God-in an earthen vessel], sinned and death was the result of that, but Jesus Who is the Son of God did not sin [the firstborn from the dead (Col. 1:18)]. He has restored life to all who believe on His name (1 Cor. 15:45-47). Therefore, dying as the Spotless Lamb of God and being raised from the dead— bringing redemption and eternal life to God's people.

> *iii.* Eliphaz the Temanite stated this question to Job: "*How much less that which is abominable and corrupt, a man who drinks iniquity like water*" (Job 15:16; Amp)?

This statement is part of a rebuttal to Job's many questions, but Eliphaz's question does not comfort Job, because Job was a righteous man who avoided, escaped and eluded evil (Job 1:1). He dedicated his entire life to pleasing

God—even if he thought there was sin present around him he would repent and ask God's forgiveness (Job 1:5). However, this question has merit when it comes to sinful humanity. It is true that they seem to drink *"iniquity like water."* It appears that in our present day society, people are more vulnerable to that *"which is abominable and corrupt"* than that which is acceptable and pleasing to God.

iv. *"For we have all become like one who is unclean [ceremonially, like a leper], and all our righteousness (our best deeds of rightness and justice) is like filthy rags or a polluted garment; we all fade like a leaf, and our iniquities, like the wind, take us away [far from God's favor, hurrying us toward destruction]. And no one calls on Your name and awakens and bestirs himself to take and keep hold of You; for You have hidden Your face from us and have delivered us into the [consuming] power of our iniquities"* (Isaiah 64: 6-7; Amp; cf. Psalms 14:3; 53:3).

Even though Isaiah is addressing Israel as a whole [including himself], these scriptures speak directly to humankind in general (for every generation), because we all have sinned. Salvation is *the gift of God* (Eph. 2:8; John 4:10) to a lost world and Jesus is the final sacrifice [as the Spotless Lamb of God] to remove sin from us forever through His divine shed blood. It is my prayer that we repent and get things right before it's too late, because just as He turned ancient Israel over to their sins, He will likewise do us the same (Rom.1: 26ff). One thing must be understood—ministry is one thing and righteous living is another. It is better that we do not give our bodies to be burned (1 Cor. 13), but give ourselves over to a consecrated dedicated, sacrificial life which is far more rational, practical and pleasing to God (Rom. 12: 1).

Chapter Six

Going to Church
and
Having Church
Verses
Being the Church

First of all I guess we need to look at the etymology of this popular word and it origin—"Church." But, before we do that, it is clear that when one hears the word *church* they think of a building in a neighborhood or on a street corner. It is a place where people go and celebrate and worship God, it is God's house or where believers meet God. Thus, this is first and for most in the minds of most people when they hear the word *church*. In this church there is a hierarchy of clergy and then laymen who follow the teachings of the clergy. There are social activities for various groups and different auxiliaries that are set in place to promote membership participation and interaction. This place called Church is where people find God and support with a family atmosphere to assist them in everyday life.

Etymology of the Word "Church"

Now, let's take a look at the etymology of "Church." **Greek:** *kyriake (oikia), kyriakon doma* "Lord's (house)" (http://etymonline.com/index.php?allowed_in_frame= 0&search=church&searchmode=none)--the Temple of God, Cathedral, [a place of worship] is emphasized in some New Testament translations. The other Greek word used for *church* that is well known in most Christian circles is *ekklēsia* [ek *(from out of or out from)* +kaleō *(to call out or to call out by name)*] (see Blue Letter Bible- Lexicon website). As we can see these Greek words for *church* are not the same in their etymological meaning. So how did this come about that the word *church* should have two different meanings? First of all let's make one thing clear, the word church has only one original meaning and that is "Lord's (house)"— this came about during the time of Constantine's reign as emperor of Rome (A.D. 306-337). Even though the word *church* itself was not used like it is used today in our present time—it was Constantine that moved Christian into the churches *kyriake (oikia), kyriakon doma* (or houses of God sort of speak). Rome was a place of many heathen gods and goddesses with their shrines and temples, however, the Christians were being persecuted.

Thus, Constantine put an end to the persecution and claimed that he was a Christian himself [however, it is not believed that he was ever converted—there is no record of his conversion]. It is he who made the order of what we call church today. Everyone going to a building to worship like the heathens did with their idolatrous temples. The first, second and early third century Christians worshiped, prayed and fellowshipped in believer's homes (Romans 16: 3-5; Acts 12: 11-12) and wherever they could find a meeting place—whether on a river's bank (Acts 16:13) or in an upper rooms (Acts 1:13; 20:7-12), they would worship, praise and teach the glad tidings of the Gospel. Their emphasis was not on a building or a house of worship, but on the people and to further advance the kingdom of God (Matt. 28: 19-20; Acts 1: 8).

God has never intended that his people should build Him a house of worship. There is only one time in the Bible that God gave instruction for His presence to be in a place, and that is when he instructed Moses to build Him the Ark of the Covenant in which he would place it in a tent (also known as the Tent of Meeting or the Tabernacle—see Exodus 25-27). Thus approximately, 440 years later God saw in the heart of King David that he wanted to build Him a house (temple) and God honored him because he was a man after God's own heart (1 Samuel 13: 14; Acts 13:22). However, God would not allow David to build the Temple himself because blood was on his hands, due to much killing in the wars he fought.

As we can see here, definitely, it was not in the heart of God for His people to build a temple for his presence, but it was in the heart of a man that He honored and loved, [King David]. This would be the only manmade shrine in historicity that God would allow [the latter temples would be houses not made with human hands (Acts 7:48; 17: 24; 1 Cor. 6:19]. This is what God said to David through His prophet Nathan,

> *"Shall you build Me a house in which to dwell? For I have not dwelt in a house since I brought the Israelites out of Egypt to this day, but have moved about with a tent for My dwelling. In all the places where I have moved with all the Israelites, did I speak a word to any from the tribes of Israel whom I commanded to be shepherd of My people Israel, asking, Why do you not build Me a house of cedar? So now say this to My servant David, Thus says the Lord of hosts: I took you from the pasture, from following the sheep, to be prince over My people Israel. And I was with you wherever you went, and have cut off all your enemies from before you; and I will make you a great name, like [that] of the great men of the earth. And I will appoint a place for My people Israel and will plant them, that they may dwell in a place of their own and be moved no more. And wicked men shall afflict*

them no more, as formerly And as from the time that I appointed judges over My people Israel; and I will cause you to rest from all your enemies. Also the Lord declares to you that He will make for you a house: And when your days are fulfilled and you sleep with your fathers, I will set up after you your offspring who shall be born to you, and I will establish his kingdom. He shall build a house for My Name [and My Presence], and I will establish the throne of his kingdom forever" (2 Samuel 7: 6-13; Amp).

Ministrant (Deacon) Stephen made this statement in Acts 7: 48-49 before his martyrdom about God not dwelling in temples and houses:

"However, the Most High does not dwell in houses and temples made with hands; as the prophet says, Heaven [is] My throne, and earth the footstool for My feet. What [kind of] house can you build for Me, says the Lord, or what is the place in which I can rest?" [Amp; cf. Isaiah 66: 1]

After reading these verses of scripture we see God's case is made—building manmade temples, (houses of God or houses of gods and goddess) were never commanded by God or His intent for the Christian assemblies (*ekklēsia*). This is the will of humanity and the ways of mankind plain and simple. The church era started by Emperor

Constantine, changed Christendom for the worst, because in our modern times Christian Leaders are more concerned about the building of Temples, Cathedrals, and church facilities more than they are for the well being of the people who attend such places. They have special offerings called "the building fund" and they have other fundraisers and offerings—constantly taking money from the people to fix-up the building as well as build new buildings that are not needed—stating, "We are God's children and we deserve the best, because we are children of the King."

The King James Bible's Deliberate Misinterpretation of Ekklesia

Between 1604 and 1611 the King of England, James I along with Bishop Richard Bancroft had a new version of the Bible written with fifteen specific rules set in place (see website http://www.sovereignword.org/index.php/king-james-bible-qextrasq/268-richard-bancrofts-rules-to-be-observed-in-the-translation-of-the-bible- [to get an observation of all fifteen rules]). The *third rule* was for the word Congregation (assembly) to not replace the old ecclesiastical word Church. This would be a direct intentional misinterpretation or mistranslation in scripture, because the original Greek interpretation is *ekklēsia*.

The early Christians before c.300 never used *ekklēsia* (assembly, congregation) for the word *church [kyriake (oikia)], kyriakon doma]*, and the word *church* was never mentioned in scripture to replace the word assembly/congregation (*ekklēsia*). **In other words Jesus and the apostles never used the word <u>church</u> in the New Testament as associated with building God an earthly physical house and putting people in it for worship and social activities (bold emphasized).** Wow! What a revelation! The original Greek translation is ekklēsia (ἐκκλησία) which is also in line with the Hebrew words qahal (*kaw-hal'*), qehillâh (*keh-hil-law'*) and `edah (*ay-daw'*) for assembly, congregation (or convocation)—*multitude.* As we can see mankind has tampered with the scriptures to emphasis the physical building structure (lord's house or master's home—secular terms) instead of the people being called out or called out by name to the community/kingdom of God and Christ as their King and Good Shepherd of the Lord's elected/selected saints—His sheep (John 10:14-16, 27).

Therefore, when we read Matthew 16:18 with the *ekklēsia* translation one can see that the scripture has a whole different and fulfilling meaning then the word *church.* King James **I** had authority over the church buildings because these buildings were operated by the state or as we say "*state run*"—keeping the people who gather in those buildings under state control or hierarchal rulership. He and Bishop Bancroft would not allow the word *church* to be removed in their new translation—which was not in line with William Tyndale's version of the bible (whose final writings and revisions were between 1526-1535)—Tyndale use the original Greek translation *ekklēsia* [assembly, in English].

We are an Individual Temple, Sanctuary (Church) Not Made with Human Hands

Even though the word *church* is mysteriously laced in paganism, its secular meaning derived from the Greek words *kyriake (oikia), kyriakon doma*. The Old English word for church is *cirice* or *circe* [derived from the West Germanic word *kirika*] which is in line with the word circus and circle or ring. It is believed that pagan worshipers would get in circles and pray to their deities. Now, with further etymological connotations understood less take a different approach to this word "Church."

Contemporary Christians today like to say, and I quote: "Let's go to church Sunday—"We had a good time at church Wednesday night"—"Bring the children to church tomorrow"—"Let's have church" or "When do y'all have church. Finally, "We really had church last night." Christians today see church as a place or an activity. A place to go and something to do [a social activity center]—it is not who the Believer is—*per se*. I believe that spiritually we as individual saints of God are temples—houses of God [our physical bodies are living sanctuaries (1 Cor. 6:19ff)], of which indwells the Holy Ghost (the Spirit of God) and we reside in Him because he is the Temple or Sanctuary of all things created [all resides in Him (Acts 17: 28], but His people (those who believe that Jesus is the Son of God) have fellowship with the FATHER through the SON intimately.

Our bodies are likening unto the Tabernacle (tent) were the Ark of the Covenant resided [or in other words the

Tabernacle is antitypical of the people of God individually].
God instructed Moses to construct the Ark and the Tent
for a place for His presence to dwell with His chosen people
(Israel)—liking unto that which is in heaven and that which
is to come. However, we have learned in scripture that our
flesh [bodies] are tents in which our souls and spirits dwell
[it is our home] were God places His Law [Word] (2 Cor.
5:1; Heb. 8: 10ff; 2 Pet. 1: 13-14; Rev. 21: 3).

Thus, God's ultimate goal and objective is to dwell
within His people as His saints [for we who believe "are His
workmanship" (2 Cor. 6:16ff; Eph. 2:10)]. Furthermore,
if we have received Jesus, His Spirit now dwells on the
inside of us communing with us individually—"Christ in
you the hope of glory" (Col. 1:26ff). That is why it is very
important that we give our bodies over to the Spirit of
God and not to the secular world—which is antagonistic
to God's righteousness. Hear the words of the apostle Paul
when he cited:

> *"Do you not know that your body is the temple (the*
> *very sanctuary) of the Holy Spirit Who lives within*
> *you, Whom you have received [as a Gift] from*
> *God? You are not your own, You were bought with*
> *a price [purchased with a preciousness and paid*
> *for, made His own]. So then, honor God and bring*
> *glory to Him in your body"* (1Cor. 6:19ff; Amp).

When God directed Moses to build the Ark of the
Covenant and place it under a tent, it was just a figure or an

antitype of what the Lord would do in the future to those who believe in His name and who were purchased by the blood of Jesus at Golgotha (*gulgōleth*) (this also includes Solomon's Temple, which was designed by King David). Paul's writing to the assembly at Corinth spells it out perfectly—touching all the salient points on this subject, when he stated:

> *"What agreement [can there be between] a temple of God and idols? For we are the temple of the living God; even as God said, I will dwell in and with and among them and will walk in and with and among them, and I will be their God, and they shall be My people. So, come out from among [unbelievers], and separate (sever) yourselves from them, says the Lord, and touch not [any] unclean thing; then I will receive you kindly and treat you with favor, And I will be a Father to you, and you shall be My sons and daughters, says the Lord Almighty"* (2 Cor. 6:16ff; Amp; cf. Heb. 8: 6-10; Jer. 31:31-33).

Since God is disclosing that He is now indwelling in His people and no longer in a manmade temple (or tabernacle). Why are we so overly concerned about a *church building* made with human hands? We run to this building thinking that we are going to get in the presence of the Lord, when the Lord should be residing in us and us in Him. God is ever present with His *ekklesia*. The Hebrew writer gives us this consolation and reassurance:

> *"Let your character or moral disposition be free from love of money [including greed, avarice, lust, and craving for earthly possessions] and be satisfied with your present [circumstances and with what you have]; for He [God] Himself has said, I will not in any way fail you nor give you up nor leave you without support. [I will] not, [I will] not, [I will] not in any degree leave you helpless nor forsake nor let [you] down (relax My hold on you)! [Assuredly not!] So we take comfort and are encouraged and confidently and boldly say, The Lord is my Helper; I will not be seized with alarm [I will not fear or dread or be terrified]. What can man do to me"* (Heb. 13:5-6; Amp)?

Jesus told His disciples that He would not leave us comfortless, and the Holy Spirit would be our instructor or educator, as well as leading or showing us the way into all truth (John 14: 26; 16: 1-14)—managing and overseeing our lives if we allow Him to assist us. Thus as you can see, this is based on fidelity and trust in Jesus—it is your choice (volition) if you want the Holy Spirit to assist you. In this hour of degeneration God's people need to come out of *church* and walk as living temples of the Holy Ghost, because lost human beings can't see God in His people.

Therefore, they will have unambiguous hope that God exists through Jesus the Messiah (the Christ of God). Stop putting emphasis on human structures made from earthly material and put our emphasis on humanity made in the image of God. We must teach people about their God and stop putting entertainment and amusements before attempting to divulge God's truths. The building should be a meeting place only [not church], not the house of God or the Lord's house, because God never commanded the New Testament Christians to build temples, cathedrals, shines, and chapels for Him. Nor did He advocate social activities, church auxiliary programs, services with programs and bucket passing offerings (which include tithing, freewill and building fund offerings).

This was never intended to be the Lord's will, nor should this be present among us [those who believe]. This should not be our top priority in godly Christian fellowships. We have gotten away from Jesus' instructions and are now in error—following after the ways of humanity and secularism. American Christian Leaders and others around the world must stop spreading the New Gospel call, "Financial Prosperity," and stop making the scripture line-up with their fictional uninspired (not from God) philosophies and line-up with the truths of the unadulterated Gospel that is able to save our souls from hell and destruction.

Chapter Seven

A Finale Word

On

This Degenerated Hour

In Which We Live

Judgment Shall Begin in the Household of God

> *"For the time [has arrived] for judgment to begin with the household of God; and if it begins with us, what will [be] the end of those who do not respect or believe or obey the good news (the Gospel) of God? And if the righteous are barely saved, what will become of the godless and wicked?" [1 Pet. 4: 17-18; Amp]*

As we can see here the household of God are the believers in Christ. If the people of God [those who are called saints and walking in habitual fellowship with Him] are scarcely or almost not saved—then what does this tell us? This tells us that God's merciful loving kindness is ineffable and indefinable. Those who profess salvation should be more than grateful to Jesus for His faithfulness, and enduring the cross and His powerful resurrection. Therefore, without Him dying for all sinners and rising up to newness of life (Rom. 6: 1-6), none of us would have hope or a chance for eternal life because all humanity has sinned and rebelled against the Lord of glory (Rom. 3:23; 5: 12).

Many of us in Christendom live like this earth is our final resting place. We may say that we can't wait to get to heaven and see Jesus, but our actions beg to differ. We are proving ourselves to be bad examples of Christianity on earth, because on our jobs we tend to not show our Christ likeness. Many of us use profanity, lie, mistreat our fellow co-workers and do whatever we can to climb up the corporate ladder to financial success. Thus, when you get the big job promotion you say that the Lord has prospered me or God has blessed me; this is the favor of the Lord, when in reality, it was your undermined and underhanded schemes, tactics and obsequious sycophantic behavior (*brown-noising*) that got you your promotion in the first place.

Furthermore, at the *so-called* church your behavior has not changed, you are still stepping on people to be close to the *so-called* church leaders (pastors). And the *so-called* pastors like you because you are successful and you tithe and give various offerings from your wealth into good ground [that is why you are so prosperous—of course this is what they tell you and the people that attend the local church]. I am so tired of all the counterfeit (play-acting) of today's *so-called* Christians.

That is why today's society can't see God in His people because the *so-called* Christians are living a life that is not conducive to holy living nor do they seem to fear the Lord God [that they say they serve]. Don't they realize that God is able to save their souls from death and in His mighty wrath He is also able to cast their bodies into a burning Hell (Luke 12:5)? You would think they would know this since they claim that they read the Bible. All the divisions in Christianity have ruined the Ekklesia (*Congregations*) and the word *church*—in its misuse has help aid in this debacle.

The Honesty and Courage of William Tyndale

The sixteenth century was a very important era for biblical interpretation. From 1526 to 1557 A.D. people in England began desiring English Bibles [which was against the law in the early 1500's]. In the month of February, 1526 in Rhine to Worms, Germany, William Tyndale (1494-1536) published the first English New Testament in spite of King Henry the VIII's vendetta against it—due to papal rule. He later published the Pentateuch in Antwerp, Belgium in January of 1530. Even though he did not get the chance to complete an Old Testament English translation, his English Pentateuch and New Testament translation became very popular in England.

This persuaded King Henry the VIII to a possible compromise with Tyndale. However, Tyndale never got a chance to meet with the King, because in Antwerp he was betrayed by an *overzealous* appalling young man from England named Henry Phillip [claiming to have papal authority], turned Tyndale in to the Antwerp authorities, and sixteen months later, on October 06, 1536, William Tyndale was executed on a stake; strangled and then burned. Thus, after his death his colleague and associate John Rogers completed the Old Testament English translation, combining the Tyndale's New Testament Translation [which was published the year after Tyndale's execution] to produce the first Tyndale English Bible. However, Rogers used an alias, "Thomas Matthew" instead so that the Tyndale name would not be recognized—he named the book, "Matthew's Bible," because John Rogers was regarded as heretical in England because of his association and friendship with William Tyndale. [The Life of William Tyndale, DeCoursey webpage; *EEB* website, *MB*—Full Story; by M. J. Epler]

The Church Error

William Tyndale never used the word *church* in his translation. He was a man of integrity that wanted the English reader to have an unequivocal translation of the Hebrew and the Greek from the Holy Scriptures. He had no hidden agendas to beguile the masses, and he was dedicated to revealing the truth of God's word in English. However, by 1556 Protestants and the Catholics were very high on a "universal church," and Theodore Beza a Presbyterian Calvinist would be the first to use the word "church" instead of assembly or congregation to solidify a hierarchal form of church government to rule universally. As we can see this was human ideals not godly intervention.

Therefore, in 1557 William Whittingham caught on to Theodore Beza's "usage of" the word *church* and produced the "first edition of the Geneva Bible." Not only this Bible, but also the Bishops Bible and later the King James Bible (1611 A.D.) would follow suit [see http://www. bible-truth.org/Ekklesia.html; http://www.britannica.com/ EBchecked/topic/63792/Theodore-Beza]. The popularity of the word *church* began to grow over time and the word *assembly* became ancillary and weakened in its relevancy in scripture. Putting the word church/churches in place of the word assembly/assemblies is a travesty, because the two words are not related in any way. Thereby using the word *church* in the Holy Scriptures, we see that it takes out of context the true meaning and intent for the Christian reader. Also this word *church* has aided in the division of Christendom with its hierarchy of various organizations and denominations with a universal concept of a worldwide presiding leader. This is not what Jesus desired or taught His *Ekklesia*.

Is Satan Winning?

Since we live in a degenerated hour, it appears that no matter how someone is living their lifestyle and calling themselves Christians, no one is willing to stand up and say the words of the apostle Paul when he cited,

> *"So, come out from among [unbelievers], and separate (sever) yourselves from them, says the Lord, and touch not [any] unclean thing; then I will receive you kindly and treat you with favor, And I will be a Father to you, and you shall be My sons and daughters, says the Lord Almighty"* (2 Cor. 6:17ff; Amp).

We live in an hour were Christian leaders are afraid to take on this world system by which Satan is prince (Eph. 2:1-3). They are afraid of what people may say about them and they are afraid that if they speak the truth they will lose members and financial offerings of support in their *so-called* churches and ministries. So they are compromising and giving in to sin in the name of financial security and prosperity. Therefore I ask this question; "are the gates of hell prevailing or triumphing in this hour of degeneration?" Jesus said in Matthew 16: 18:

> *"And I also say to thee, that thou art a rock, and upon this rock I will build my assembly, and gates of Hades shall not prevail against it"* (YLT).

The gates of Hell are supposed to be no match for the assembly (*ekklesia*) of Jesus. Satanic domination and influence should not be an issue or a factor with God's people—even though there will be tribulations in this life (2 Thess. 1: 4)—we have overcome the devil by the Blood of the Lamb and our confession of Jesus as Messiah and Savior (John 16:33; 1 John: 2: 12-14; 4:4). So why is the *so-called* church experiencing degeneration? The answer is clearly defined, from the third century of Christian history till now, we have seen error, after error, after error—divisions (not unity) and manmade fictions and fabrications leading the way with their *church* doctrines and mission statements instead of the unadulterated word of God.

However, today's Gospel that is being preached is not the Gospel of Jesus and the apostles. We must drop our manmade doctrines and embellished cliché's and remove the emphasis on manmade buildings with hierarchy rulership. Thus, we must become *true* shepherds who are really mingling with and resembling the sheep (God's people). We must stop being humanities' clergy and start being humble servants to the people, teaching them (the saints) to do the work of the ministry by example (Eph. 4: 12). Thus the Aaronic priesthood (Levitical priesthood of the Old Testament), was just a figure or symbolic of the antitype **Saints of God** (the *ekklesia*) of the future. Peter makes this unambiguous statement that substantiates this:

> "*But you are a chosen race, a royal priesthood, a dedicated nation, [God's] own purchased, special*

> *people, that you may set forth the wonderful deeds*
> *and display the virtues and perfections of Him Who*
> *called you out of darkness into His marvelous light"*
> (1 Peter 2:9; Amp).

Therefore, let us stop wearing fancy priestly clothing and collars [looking like kings on thrones], Jesus and the apostles never did that nor advocated this—it was the Pharisees that wore similar types of clothing—trying to look important (Luke 20: 46). Now can be the hour of integrity, honesty and regeneration, not deterioration— revitalizing back to the *naked* (pure) word of God. We must tell the people the truth [without embellishments]. Truth brings liberty and the people have been in bondage far too long, due to our failures and being misguided for so many years (John 8: 32; c.f. 2 Cor. 3: 17; Gal. 5: 1). We must take heed to the Spirit of God and get our houses in order [this means every individual that calls themselves Christians before time runs out].

The Institution of Holy Matrimony Is Deteriorating

In this hour of degeneration we see that many heterosexual people are not concerned much about marrying anymore. When couples unite with one another, their preferences are to live together [also known as *shaking-up or shaking*]. Even though these couples call themselves Christians and attend the local *so called* church they have no fear of God that they are wrong in anyway. One would think to make all of this wrong right they would marry to stop burning in their passion for one another. This is what the apostle Paul had to say about the unmarried couples:

> *"But if they have not self-control (restraint of their passions), they should marry. For it is better to marry than to be aflame [with passion and tortured continually with ungratified desire]"* (1 Cor. 7: 9; Amp).

Paul is giving this admonition so that we as Christians would honor God and fear Him [this is wisdom]. It is a known fact that when heterosexual couples live together they have no intention of a long term relationship that is free from other outside sexual partners. A lot of times when couples have disagreements or arguments, they separate or leave for a while and have sexual relations with other people.

They may return to the former partner or move in with the new partner that may offer something better than the former partner had to offer. However, how can anyone say that they are a child of God living like this? We must show these people what God's word says and get this *error* corrected. Either they will stop their foolishness or go on in their folly. It is our responsibility as people of God to tell all people the truth; to bring glory and honor to Jesus' name.

Unholy Matrimony

The rise of rights for Sodomites and Lesbians has caused a debate in the world of whether the same-sex can marry.

Why are people so surprised that this should happen? Satan is the ruler of this world system, and just like in the times of Noah (just before the deluge) marriage was major and very important (Matt. 24: 37-39). However, in our modern times same-sex marriage is on the rise around the world being promoted by media and government. Let me make this statement before expounding any further on this subject:

> *"No one is born a Sodomite or a Lesbian. People chose to have same sex partners and sexual relations with them [whether forced (raped) or consensual]. This is the will and act of humans; not the will or desires of God. Having sex is a choice—no one has to have sex with anyone—people choose to have sex. This behavior [same sex relations] is not acceptable and it is ruining people's lives. It is the spirit of this world's system [Satan and demon powers] that are pressing and pushing the homosexual same-sex agendum around the world. James made it clear to us when he cited and I paraphrase: "Commit your life and be a slave to godliness (be the Lord's subject's only) and give great resistance to the spirits of darkness—refusing them (Satan and demonic powers). Be very antagonistic against this world's system in which Satan is prince and the Devil will leave you alone".* (James 4:7).

Unholy matrimony is now being accepted in the *so called* churches as well. This should let true Christians know that the so called *church* is not the way; Jesus is the Way the Truth and the Life (John 14: 6). He is our King and Chief Apostle [The Bishop of our souls], not some manmade hierarchy presiding over same-sex unholy matrimony [calling it a "modern family"]. Also these mega *so called* church leaders are not standing-up against this, because they have many Sodomites and Lesbians in their organizations, and they are afraid of media attacks, loosing donations (offerings, tithes) and book sales. They market themselves daily in front of people all around the world making a lot of money. So they compromise with the world and are very careful when dealing with the media to avoid a barrage of attacks.

These abominations are definite signs of the end-times or "the last days." Paul prognosticated these times with precise accuracy in 2 Timothy 3: 1-5:

> *"But understand this, that in the last days will come (set in) perilous times of great stress and trouble [hard to deal with and hard to bear]. For people will be lovers of self and [utterly] self-centered, lovers of money and aroused by an inordinate [greedy] desire for wealth, proud and arrogant and contemptuous boasters. They will be abusive (blasphemous, scoffing), disobedient to parents, ungrateful, unholy and profane. [They will be] without natural [human] affection (callous and inhuman), relentless (admitting of no truce or appeasement); [they will be] slanderers (false accusers, troublemakers), intemperate and loose in*

> *morals and conduct, uncontrolled and fierce, haters*
> *of good [They will be] treacherous [betrayers], rash,*
> *[and] inflated with self-conceit. [They will be]*
> *lovers of sensual pleasures and vain amusements*
> *more than and rather than lovers of God. For*
> *[although] they hold a form of piety (true religion),*
> *they deny and reject and are strangers to the power*
> *of it [their conduct belies the genuineness of their*
> *profession]. Avoid [all] such people [turn away from*
> *them]"* (Amp).

Notice that Paul admonishes that we who truly fear the Lord should totally evade "such people" and have nothing to do with them. Therefore, the reverence for our Lord Jesus and what He stood for while walking the earth in His corporeal state is being disrespected, belittled and disparaged. Righteousness, godliness, sanctification, true holiness, faith and hope in Jesus, seems to now be insignificant. However, the words *love* and *judge* are being used out of context to cover unholy matrimony when God hold all homosexual activity as strange (unnatural) or liking unto strange flesh (Jude 1: 7; Rom. 1: 26ff; c.f. 1 Cor. 6: 9ff). Men, don't allow satanic femininity in your life; you must resist the devil when he sends the spirit of sodomy to you. You must allow your masculinity to dominate—giving in to it, because this is the will of the Lord for your life. Women you must do likewise (or the same response as men), by giving in to your femininity and disallowing (forbidding) satanic same sex virility (trying to be masculine) in your life. By doing so, you will be pleasing in the sight of the Lord.

They Are Perishing-A Call for Restoration

If we don't wake-up and tell the truth many are going to perish. Many have already perished and some a perishing even as I write this book and as you read these pages. We must stop what we are doing because it is not working. The people are giving up because they can't see God in the people. They feel like there is no alternative and there is no hope. Curtis Mayfield, a very famous R&B musician in the 1950's through the 1970's said this in a song "(Don't Worry)If there's hell below we're all gonna go" [this also is the title of the song].

This song to me is a cry for help to God, because it appears that Mr. Mayfield has no hope [because he can't see God in the people—so all are lost]. Like Les McCann and Eddie Harris' 'Trying to Make it Real Compared to What! [See chapter 3 pp.53-54] If there ever was a time, now is that time, to get it right with God through Jesus the Messiah and do the best that we can [as fellow workmen] to assist God in delivering a lost dying degenerating world (1 Cor. 3: 9). If we say we love God we will obey Him (John 14:15; 15:10) and work with Him to get this done. This is the hour of degeneration [and there is no doubt about that], however, we the people of God, must repent of our degradations and sinful disgraces and awaken from ignorance, and come alive again unto godly wisdom—changing this contemporary time *in which we live* into THE HOUR OF REGENERATION, RESTORATION AND REVIVIFICATION (Please read Eph 5: 14-20).

:: Closing Statement

From the 1970's till now, Satan has sent two waves of deceptions that has moved Christendom deeper into apostasy: (1) **Ikeism**: The Right Reverend Ike's "Thinkenomics"—the *"name it and claim it"* movement—which transferred to the Christian Prosperity Movement or the Prosperity Gospel of the 1980's—lead by Oral Roberts with his "Seed Faith Giving." (2.) **The Gospel of Inclusion:** Satan's repulsive push for Sodomites and Lesbians also know as (LGBT) to be accepted as Christians.

With their *Queen James* version of the Bible and Gay Churches building up in the United States (like Gay bars), we can see that this movement is really gaining momentum and it want be long before many of the mega churches and mainstream denominational churches accept these reprobates; stating "we must have compassion and don't judge them, we must show love to them and not be homophobic—isn't this what Jesus would do?" These are words of deception, by which once again Satan is beguiling humanity (See Gen. 3). It is now time, I mean high time for Christians to get out of church (leave it) and go to Jesus Who is the Author and Finisher of our faith.

Paul made this statement about the end-time apostasy in 2 Thessalonians 2: 3:

"Let no one deceive or beguile you in any way, for that day will not come except the apostasy comes first [unless the predicted great falling away of those who have professed to be Christians has come], and the man of lawlessness (sin) is revealed, who is the son of doom (of perdition)" [Amp].

Many are falling from the faith and are accepting every wind and doctrine that is being preached without questioning the ones spitting out these heresies in this hour of degeneration. We who are taking a stand against these heresies are very few and we have no mega platform. However, I am sounding the alarm everywhere that I can, to admonish the people to live godly and holy and put their trust in the unadulterated word of God (**The Bible**). Read the Bible and accept it as it is—it is not outdated nor is it human inspired. It is God breathed (2 Tim. 3:16) and our *only* hope for this HOUR OF DEGENERATION.

THE END

Bibliography

Blue Letter Bible- Lexicon [s.a] *Ekklesia: Root Word (Etymology) G1537 & G2564*: Retrieved from the BLBL website: http://www.blueletterbible. org/lang/lexicon/ lexicon. cfm?Strongs=G1577&t=KJV

Christian Classics Ethereal Library (n.d.). *Early Church Fathers by Richardson, C.C (1909-1976). Selections from the Work Against Heresies by Irenaeus, Bishop of Lyons: "The Refutation and Overthrow of the Knowledge Falsely So Called" The Text: (Book I) The Heretics: 358 Preface: 360 The Faith of the Church second paragraph :* Retrieved from the CCEL website: http://www.ccel.org/ccel/ richardson/fathers.xi.i.iii.html

DeCoursey, Christina & Matthew [s.a.] *The Life of William Tyndale.* Retrieved from DeCoursey's webpage: http://www.tyndale.org/DeCoursey/life.html

Encyclopaedia Britannica [s.a] *Theodore Beza.* Retrieved From the Editors of EB website: http://www.britannica.com/EBchecked/topic/63792/Theodore-Beza

Epler, M.J.©2012. *Matthew Bible (Full Story)—Early English Bibles:* Massillon, OH, USA. Retrieved from the Early English Bible website: http://massillonchurches.com/BibleSites/earlyversions/MatthewFull4b.html

Harper, Douglas© 2001-2013. *Online Etymology Dictionary: Degenerate*: Retrieved from the OED website: http://www.etymonline.com/index.php?term=degenerate

_____ 2001-2013b. *Online Etymology Dictionary: Church.* Retrieved from the OED website: http://etymonline.com/index.php?allowed_in_frame=0&search=church&searchmode=none

Huus, Kari (2012). *Atheists Bill Big Names for 'Coming Out' Party in Capital.* Retrieved from US News on NBC.com website: http://usnews.nbcnews.com/_news/2012/02/16/10429346-atheists-bill-big-names-for-coming-out-party-in-capital?lite

Joyner, Twyman P. (2012). *His Mighty Word of Power: [Chapter 3 "Yom" Genesis 1:3ff; p.25].* Bloomington, Indiana: WestBow Press a division of Thomas Nelson ISBN 978-1-4497-6109-7

Kirby, Peter © 2001-2012. *Polycarp: The Epistle of Polycarp Translated by J.B. Lightfoot: Polycarp 2:1.* Retrieved from Early Christian Writings website: http://www.earlychristianwritings.com/text/polycarp-lightfoot.html

McCann, Les & Harris, Eddie (1969). *Compared To What lyrics.* Retrieved from Smartlyrics.com website: http://www.smartlyrics.com/Song606746-Les-McCann--Eddie-Harris-Compared-To-What-lyrics.aspx

Ray, Fredrick K. [s.a.] *Meat Curing: Curing Ingredients.*
Oklahoma Cooperative Extension Services ANSI-3994.
Division of Agricultural Science and Natural Resources-
Oklahoma State University. Retrieved from Okstate.
edu website: http://pods.dasnr.okstate.edu/docushare/
dsweb/Get/Document-2055/ANSI-3994web.pdf

The American Heritage® Dictionary of the English
Language, Fourth Edition copyright ©2000 by
Houghton Mifflin Company. Updated in 2009.
Published by Houghton Mifflin Company. All rights
reserved. *Various word definitions, encyclopedia and
etymology* all retrieved from The Free Dictionary by
Farlex website: http://www.thefreedictionary.com/
domain

The Lockman Foundation copyright© 1954, 1958, 1962,
1964, 1965, 1987. Biblegateway. Joshua 24 Amplified
Bible: *J. R. Miller, Devotional Hours with the Bible on
Joshua 24:20; on the subject of idols.* Retrieved from
Biblegateway.com
website: http://www.biblegateway.com/
passage/?search=joshua%2024&version=AMP

Stewart, David. [s.a.] *Discussions with my Friend: An
Introduction to the Gospel of Jesus Christ: Chapter 22:
The Christian Apostasy : Loss of Apostolic Leadership and
Revelation. 2nd Paragraph.* Retrieved from Cumorah.

com website: http://www.cumorah.com/index.
php?target=outreach_articles&story_id=10

Sovereign Word (nd.). *Richard Bancroft's Rules for translating the King James Bible (1604)*: Rule #3 emphasized: Retrieved from Sovereign Word website: www.sovereignword.org/index.php/king-james-bible-qextrasq/268-richard-bancrofts-rules-to-be-observed-in-the-translation-of-the-bible- [to view all fifteen rules to observe]